The Newer, More English Version

The Newer, More English Version

Tom Carver

BOOKS

Winchester, UK
Washington, USA

First published by iff Books, 2013
iff Books is an imprint of John Hunt Publishing Ltd., Laurel House, Station Approach,
Alresford, Hants, SO24 9JH, UK
office1@jhpbooks.net
www.johnhuntpublishing.com
www.iff-books.com

For distributor details and how to order please visit the 'Ordering' section on our website.

Text copyright: Tom Carver 2012

ISBN: 978 1 84694 711 7

A CIP catalogue record for this book is available from the British Library.

Design: Lee Nash

Printed and bound by CPI Group (UK) Ltd, Croydon, CR0 4YY

We operate a distinctive and ethical publishing philosophy in all
areas of our business, from our global network of authors to
production and worldwide distribution.

CONTENTS

Genesis

Genesis I

In the beginning was the singularity, and the singularity was infinitely dense and infinitely hot,

And the singularity expanded and the singularity cooled and there was chaos,

And of the primeval atom was born the Universe.

And the Universe was matter and antimatter, and baryogenesis was violated and matter annihilated antimatter until only matter remained,

And matter resolved into hydrogen, and after hydrogen came helium and deuterium and all elements,

And with elements came mass and with mass came gravity,

And gravity caused gas clouds to form into stars and planets and moons,

And gravity caused planets to revolve around stars, and moons around planets,

And on some planets the elements manifested as water and as earth, and there were seas and lands and atmosphere,

And the orbit of planets cast days and nights and the orbit of moons pulled tides, and of the imperfection of orbits sprung seasons,

And of the chemistry on one particular planet, and maybe others also, came nucleic acids, and nucleic acids were good.

Now nucleic acids were unlike other molecules, and nucleic acids were loosely replicable,

And in the disorder and the richness on the earth the nucleic acids became numerous,

And the nucleic acids all were different.

And of the chemistry also came proteins and proteins too were unlike other molecules,

And some proteins encased and some protected and some catalysed nucleic acids, and it was good.

And from the proteins and the nucleic acids and the symbiosis thereof was borne life.

And each life needed raw material to replicate, and those with most raw material became most common,

And as time passed and generations of lifes came and went simplifications and complexities arose by chance,

And some garnered more raw material and some garnered less and the fittest survived.

And in time life begat ur-cells and those ur-cells lived and replicated and evolved through luck and circumstances,

And of those ur-cells came photoynthesisers and fungi and algae and all sorts,

And by the same force multiple celled constructs arose and flourished and in time all forms of squirming masses and photosynthesisers.

And so in time from the first nucleic acid came animals that lived on the land and those that lived in the air, and plants that lived in the sea and plants that lived on the land, and all forms of complications and devices permitted.

But as the lifes thrived a terrible event did come to pass, and ninety-five of every hundred of the species of creatures then alive were destroyed.

But the squirming masses and photosynthesisers did recover, and the ecosystem did rebuild, and the dinosaurs did have dominion.

And as the climate shifted and niches moved, birds and

mammals and grass did evolve and dinosaurs extinguished.

And of the multitude did emerge an ur-hominid, whose seed would come to have dominion over the fish of the sea and over the fowl of the air and over every living thing that moveth.

Genesis 2

And in Eden, at the head of the Euphrates, grew plants and trees with abundant food,

And the ur-hominid gathered the fruits of the garden, and the ur-hominid ate what he wished.

But there were plants he did not wish to eat; the tree of the knowledge of good and evil he did not touch,

For the fruit of the tree of the knowledge of good and evil was known to poison and to void the primitive mind of the ur-hominid.

And the ur-hominid learned to communicate with his brethren and to name the beasts and the herbs,

And the ur-hominid learned to fashion herbs and bones and rocks according to his needs,

And the ur-hominid used his tools and his tongue to great effect and his dominion over the fish of the sea and over the fowl of the air and over the grasses and trees and herbs and every living thing that moveth increased,

And the ur-hominid learned to shape his world according to his thoughts,

And from the ur-hominid came a hominid, and it was good.

And it came to pass that the hominid dwelled together with his mate and together they gathered the fruits and hunted the beasts of the garden, and raised their offspring,

And the hominid thought the tree of the knowledge of good and evil was poison, for his forebears had suffered from it and his forebears had spoken of it.

And his mate knew of the tree of the knowledge of good and evil and his mate thought that surely it would poison her.

Genesis 3

And as the hominid learned to shape his world, so the world shaped the hominid,

And it came to pass one day that the female named Eve felt compelled to taste fruit of the tree of the knowledge of good and evil and to open her eyes and know of good and of evil,

And the male named Adam took the fruit of the tree of the knowledge of good and evil and tried it also.

And Adam and Eve were not poisoned, and Adam and Eve's minds were not rendered void,

And Adam and Eve saw visions and opened their eyes and their minds and knew they were alive, and naked.

And Adam and Eve enjoyed the fruit of the tree of the knowledge of good and evil and thenceforth they partook of it on occasion with great ceremony and great joy,

And the ceremony and joy gave unity to the man and woman and their brethren and in unity they prospered.

And with prosperity and ceremony came wise men and rituals also,

And in time man and woman's dominion over the creatures and the plants led to husbandry and tillage,

And man and woman together tilled the ground and kept sheep, and the innocence of days gone by was lost.

Genesis 3A

And on other rivers in other gardens ur-hominids lived and gathered the fruits and hunted the beasts.

And the ur-hominids learned to speak with his brethren and to give names to the beasts and herbs they ate,

And the ur-hominids learned to fashion herbs and bones and rocks according to their needs,

And the ur-hominids used their tools and their tongues to great effect and their dominion over the fish of the sea and over the fowl of the air and over the grasses and trees and herbs and over every living thing that groweth increased,

And the ur-hominids learned to shape their world according to their thoughts,

And from the ur-hominids came hominids, and it was good.

But in those other gardens on those other rivers there was no tree of the knowledge of good and evil, and those hominids kept their innocence and their minds held closed and there was no ceremony, no joy and no unity.

And they did not prosper, and it was not good.

Genesis 4

And of the original man and woman descended two distinct families,

And Cain's family tilled the ground, and Abel's family kept sheep, and by this division these families grew distant and rivalrous.

And they ceased to be each other's brethren and ceased to inter-breed, and instead tribalised and speciated,

And the keepers of the sheep grew in number and in strength and the tillers of the ground were afraid.

And the tillers of the ground understood that something must be done,

And the tillers of the ground invented the doctrine of pre-emptive warfare,

And the tillers of the ground attacked and slew the keepers of the sheep and destroyed their species,

And Cain's tillers of the land spread far and wide to dwell in all the lands then known, and no more had fear of the keepers of the sheep for genocide had been accomplished,

And there were recriminations and inquests as they knew pre-emptive war was wrong.

But the inquest proved nothing and Cain's tillers of the land multiplied and spread across the land,

And such were the numbers of the tillers of the land and such was the success in the tilling of the land that there was surplus production,

And surplus production meant not all the people were needed for the tilling of the land,

And, lo, those skilled in making tills stuck to making tills and did learn to barter,

And those skilled in building dwellings also bartered,

And markets were established and around the markets grew settlements.

And the city Enoch was founded, and in the unity and the excess of the city,

And in the happiness of peace after the killing of the keepers of the sheep, the tillers of the land turned their minds and hands to learning.

And the people of Enoch wished to improve their lives and the people of Enoch had surplus time and energy,

And the people of Enoch used their time and energy wisely and from the city of Enoch came forth great novelty and invention,

And as the city of Enoch grew, the keepers of the cattle were compelled to roam further for feed,

And the keepers of the cattle needed mobile shelter from the desert,

And of that need tents were formed.

And the people of Enoch roamed the land and grazed their cattle,

And the people of Enoch sat at campfires and gazed at stars and told tales and sang songs,

And the people of Enoch plucked at their bows and whistled into cups,

And in time the harp and the organ were fashioned.

And the jewellers of Enoch beat gold and silver, and that was good for decoration but not much else,

And the potters of Enoch found that green stone turned to metal in furnaces, and copper was its colour and from copper blades could be forged,

And with impurities in copper came bronze, and bronze was good also,

And then came iron, and iron was better for iron held its edge.

And such was the beginning of civilisation, and the children of Cain's tillers of the land were many and passed their days in learning and in study.

Genesis 5
And there came a third tribe, descended from Seth, and Seth's offspring were many and they also passed their days in learning and in study.

Genesis 6
And in time the renewal of the seasons was known to be the passing of a year and each year was known to be one year, and a second year made two years, a third made three and so forth,

And where once it was believed that man could live nine hundred years, life was recorded as only one hundred and twenty years,

And the ones and twos and threes became arithmetic, and

arithmetic was studied.

And using arithmetic men built ever larger tents and dwellings,
    And out of brass and iron men fashioned ever more wondrous tools and ever more complex artifices,
    And with these artifices men took pitch from the ground and trees from the woods and made dwellings that floated upon the seas.

And men used their artifices and their learning to outdo each other in resplendence and in beauty,
    And men's tents and sea-dwellings and artifices became ever more mighty and more beautiful.

And in their leisure men desired distraction and amazement,
    And men enjoyed the exotic,
    And men caught animals and kept them as spectacles,
    And men built menageries and aviaries.

And one of the children of Seth, by name of Noah, was something of a braggart,
    And Noah set out to make the largest sea-dwelling known,
    And Noah set out to make his sea-dwelling one of finery and of beauty,
    And Noah took gopher wood for his sea-dwelling,
    And Noah took pitch for his sea-dwelling.

And Noah's sea-dwelling was as grand as he could imagine,
    And Noah's sea-dwelling was five hundred feet long and eighty feet wide and fifty feet tall,
    And Noah's sea-dwelling was three stories inside and many rooms.

And Noah wished to house a menagerie in his sea-dwelling for his sea-dwelling was to be the greatest in all the land,

And Noah collected a pair of each of the animals of which he knew and housed them in his sea-dwelling,

And Noah's sea-dwelling was bedazzling and a wonder of its time, and the neighbours were impressed.

Genesis 7

And men bickered and fought and intrigued and built and learnt,

And in this fashion the civilisation continued on its path,

Until it came to pass that the civilisation was destroyed by water.

It was said that the fountains of the great deep were broken up and the windows of the heavens opened,

And it could be that the waters of the Mediterranean breached a sill,

Or the waters of the Mediterranean or of the Indian Ocean rose up,

But for sure it seems a terrible rain did fall.

And it so happened that Noah had invited Shem and Japheth and Ham and their wives to tour his sea-dwelling,

And the party was on the sea-dwelling when the waters of the flood arrived,

And there was much excitement as the sea-dwelling floated, and gloating at neighbours' misfortune.

And the rain fell forty days and forty nights,

And the land was flooded,

And the waters covered land as far as could be seen and all the budding civilisation was washed away,

And remnants of the civilisation known to Noah floated on the waters,

And the debris of the destruction was awful to behold.

And gloating turned to shame and shame to horror and despair.

But Noah's sea-dwelling floated well,

And Noah's sea-dwelling kept the waters out,

And Noah and Shem and Japheth and Ham did play many games of cards, and the families played charades.

Genesis 8

And the waters prevailed upon the earth one hundred and fifty days and longer,

And the sea-dwelling became an awful place to be,

And food became scarce and drinking water also.

And the chickens did stop laying, and the cows did stop milking,

And all around was desolation.

But Noah and his family caught fish to eat, and ate it raw,

And Noah and his family caught seaweed for the animals, and ate it also,

And Noah and his family fed animals to animals, and also ate,

And Noah and his family bled animals, and drank the blood,

And Noah and his family cut meat from animals alive, and ate.

And the waters abated little by little, and as survival beckoned the sea-dwelling felt more ark than prison,

And birds released from Noah's aviary kindled hope, returning with nestbuilding sprigs, And in time the ark came to rest in the mountains of Ararat, and Noah rejoiced,

But the mountains of Ararat held nothing for Noah and his survivors, and they were despondent,

And the waters abated further,

And the ark kept floating on the waters.

And in time the earth dried and the ark did rest upon the earth,
    And Noah and the children and the beasts and the fowls once
more walked upon the earth.

Genesis 9

And Noah thought of the destruction,
    And Noah recalled the bodies in the water, and the stench in
the air,
    And he knew it was over and Noah had survived,
    And Noah felt special and Noah felt chosen.

And Noah knew all the land he could see was his,
    And Noah knew his task was to rebuild the life lost,
    And Noah wished to rebuild it not the way it had been, for in
his reverie Noah knew the way of men had been wrong,
    And Noah knew he had survived the flood by wrongs.

And Noah knew that laws must be adopted, and standards
created,
    And Noah decreed that no more was meat to be cut from live
animals,
    And no more was animal blood to be drunk.
    And Noah decreed that any man who killed another would
himself be killed,
    And that any animal that killed a man would be killed,
    And that any man who killed himself would be cursed.
    And it came to pass that by Noah's laws his children were not
as savage as had been the children of Seth.

And Noah pondered his luck and thanked his lucky stars and
gazed at the sky, and Noah saw beautiful colours in the sky,
    And Noah, though he knew it not, saw the light of the sun

shining on the droplets of water in the cloud,

And the light of the sun was refracted on entering the droplet and reflected and refracted once more,

And the light emerged in resplendent colours as a bow in the cloud.

And Noah felt that the colours must mean something.

And Noah's children were afraid of the clouds in the sky, and Noah clocked that the colours coincided with the clouds and sun,

And Noah said unto his children, Behold the bow in the cloud and fear not, for the bow in the cloud will protect us,

And the children of Noah knew no better and the children of Noah were not afraid.

And Noah dispersed his children as far and as wide as they could go, and Noah instructed them to populate and cultivate the land,

And Noah himself took a plot and kept sheep and tilled land,

And Noah's farm grew and Noah's flocks grew and prosperity returned.

And it came to pass that Noah discovered vines and grew himself some grapes,

And Noah adored the grape.

And Noah crushed the grapes and found the juice was good,

And Noah had many grapes and much grape juice, and some he forgot about,

And when Noah found some forgotten grape juice it did smell different,

And Noah did drink it anyway,

And Noah felt unusual and Noah was amused,

And Noah drank more of the grape juice and Noah did get pissed.

And Noah felt queasy and his vision did blur and his balance did lessen,

And Noah was sick beside the door of his tent,

And Noah passed out on his bed without his clothes and without his pyjamas.

And Ham was visiting and thought it amusing,

And Ham went to his brothers Shem and Japheth and told them their father had been sick,

And Ham did tell his brothers how Noah could not stand and could not walk and could not talk,

And Ham laughed, and Shem and Japheth were horrified.

And Shem and Japheth cleared up the sick and covered their father,

And in the morning Noah hazily recalled the incident.

And Noah was not amused.

And Noah drank again the fermented grape juice and ranted and raged against his no-good son Ham and praised his pious son Shem and industrious Japheth,

And Noah beat Ham in drunken rages,

And Noah despised Ham's son Canaan and ordered that Canaan should wait upon Shem and Japheth,

And Canaan was afraid of Noah's drunken rages and he did so wait.

Genesis 10
And new tribes descended from the survivors of the flood,

And the tribes spread around the world.

Genesis 11
And for generations after the flood the tribes spoke the same language,

And the tribes travelled and founded cities,

And the tribes found they could make bricks and mortar,

And cities could be built faster and buildings taller than before,

And a famous tower was built at Babel.

And the cities developed and their cultures diverged,

And regional dialects devolved,

And it came to pass that the world was not of one language,

And the descendants of Ham and Shem and Japheth were different,

And the descendants of each of Ham and Shem and Japheth equally were different,

And hundreds of peoples and cultures and languages filled the earth.

And Japheth's line spread West to be the Caucasian Scythians, Serbs, Croats, Armenians, Welsh, Picts, Irish, Germans, Turks, Slavs, Magyars, Persians, Ionians, Tabali, Georgians, Italics, Iberians, Basques, Phrygians, Meskheti, Moschoi, Illyrians, Thracians, Etruscans, Goths and Jutes.

And Ham's line spread South to be the African Canaanites, Berbers, Toubou, Fulani, Guanches, Egyptians, Nubians, Ethiopians, Oromo, Somali and Tutsis,

And Shem's line spread East to be the Semite Akkadians, Sumerians, Assyrians, Babylonians, Eblaites, Aramaeans, Ugarites, Ammonites, Edomites, Israelites, Moabites, Phoenicians, Sabaeans, Aksumites, Liihyanites, Thamuds, Ghassanids and Nabataeans.

Genesis 12

And Terah descendant of Shem lived in Ur, and Ur was a great city, and in Ur women could be priests, and in Ur the women priests were also hookers,

And all of Ur had gods for this and gods for that,

And the wise men of Ur knew there were no gods,

But the wise men of Ur knew the god-characters entertained the people and explained a bit of pre-history,

And the wise men of Ur knew the god-characters were a potent force for controlling the people.

And Terah's son was Abram, and Terah's grandson not by Abram was Lot,

And Abram's wife was Sarai, and she also was Terah's daughter, and this was normal at the time.

And Abram and Sarai struggled for children, and Terah thought a move might do them good,

And Terah and Abram and Lot and their wives left the desert city Ur,

And Terah and Abram and Lot and their wives moved north to Haran, where the climate was better,

And still Sarai produced no children, and this did frustrate her brother-husband, who knew not that inbreeding is no good.

And in time old Terah's synapses ceased to fire and Abram became the boss.

And Abram was ambitious and Abram dreamed dreams of fame and fortune and numberless descendants,

And Haran was no place for the founding of a dynasty, nay, a nation,

And Abram knew he should leave Haran and move to a more propitious place,

And Abram heard the land of the Canaanites was fertile, and Abram wanted it and, Terah being dead, Abram set about it.

And Lot listened to Abram's dreams, and Lot wanted to stick with Abram,

And Abram replied, Well, nephew, if you must.

And Abram and Lot and their families and servants moved south to the land of the Canaanites,
And in the Samarian hills Abram wished to settle, but Canaanites were already there,
And Abram recalled the curse of Ham, and so Abram ignored the Canaanites.

Now Abram had a target and a plan, and Abram pondered how to make it happen,
And Abram recognised that success would follow solidarity, and solidarity derived from belonging,
And it followed that brand identity was a must, and clan definition was de rigueur,
And Abram had a brainwave,
And Abram built an altar for sacrifice.

But Abram's altar was unusual; Abram's altar was not to the gods of men of Ur,
And Abram's altar was not to the gods of men of Haran.
Abram's altar was to Abram's ego.

And Abram's ego was quite something, and Abram's ego told him he would found a great nation, and that he was the greatest, and that no ill would befall him, and that all those that helped him would prosper and those who stood in his way would be struck down,
For Abram understood that through unity came greatness, and a unity of worship would lead to greatness of people.

And thus Abram cast the first die of his new nation,
And Abram's nation was to be in this land of the Canaanites.

And Abram moved south to Bethel and built another altar, and by this device Abram hoped for lebensraum.

But it came to pass that Abram's ego had exaggerated, and famine struck the fledgling nation,

And forced Abram to abandon Canaan and seek refuge in Egypt.

And in Egypt the Pharaoh took a fancy to Sarai,

And such were the customs that had Abram claimed Sarai as his wife the Pharaoh might have killed him,

And such were the customs that had Abram claimed Sarai as his sister a dowry would be due,

And it seemed to Abram a no-brainer that Sarai should be his sister and not his wife,

And Abram said unto the Pharaoh not that Sarai was his wife, and Abram said that Sarai was his sister, and this was indeed the half-truth,

And Sarai lived in the house of the Pharaoh, and Sarai no doubt picked up some saucy foreign customs, and Abram picked up many sheep and oxen and asses and servants and camels and gold and silver,

And such is the life of a pimp.

But the Pharaoh caught the clap from Sarai, and the Pharaoh was not stupid, and the Pharaoh sussed out that Sarai was wife as well as sister,

And the Pharaoh sent Sarai back to Abram, and Abram out of Egypt.

Genesis 13

And Abram and Lot and their wives and servants gathered up their fortunes and went unto Bethel from whence they had come.

And Abram had prospered in Egypt and Abram returned

with many animals and many servants,

And Lot had also prospered and did also return with many animals and many servants.

And in Bethel lived already Canaanites and Perizzites, and there was much jostling for land and many skirmishes for grazing and disputes with neighbours,

And Abram felt Lot was cramping his plans, and Abram felt that Lot's sheep were drinking his animals' water and eating his animals' grass,

And Abram felt that Lot's children should not form part of Abram's nation, and Abram told Lot in no uncertain terms to bugger off,

And Lot left for the cities of the plains of Jordan, and Lot loved life in Sodom,

And Abram had the land of Canaan unto himself, forgetting the Canaanites, and forgetting the Perizzites too.

And Abram's ego once more spake and said unto him lift up thine eyes and look from the place where thou art northward and southward and eastward and westward, and ignore the peoples living here, and make it yours,

And Abram went unto Mamre and built another altar.

Genesis 14

Now Abram was only one of many patriarchs each striving for success,

And neighbouring patriarchs grouped into confederacies and went raiding for food and women and gold and silver.

And on a raid Chedorlaomer captured the king of Sodom, and Sodom with him and with Sodom, Lot and all his goods and people,

And Abram heard of his feckless nephew's capture, and Abram spotted an opportunity,

And Abram assembled three hundred and eighteen servants and gave them blades and if no blades then sticks,

And Abram did the same with servants of his confederates,

And Abram in the dead of night rushed the camp of Chedorlaomer,

And the servants of Abram and of the confederates did rush the camp also,

And all did rush from a multitude of directions, and did strike tent poles down and make much noise,

And panic did spread in the camp of Chedorloamer and men awoke knowing not what had befallen and men awoke and ran in fear,

And Abram did chase them all to Hobah and did rescue Lot and Lot's goods and women and much more besides.

And the king of Sodom and the king of Salem welcomed Abram back,

And the king of Salem gave Abram bread and wine, and the king of Salem had heard of Abram's eccentricity, and the king of Salem had heard of the ego of Abram, and the king of Salem had seen the altars built by Abram,

And the king of Salem knew to ingratiate himself with Abram,

And the king of Salem announced his priestdom of the ego of Abram, and Abram was pleased,

And Abram gave the king of Salem a tenth of the plunder from Chedorloamer's camp.

And the king of Sodom knew the rules, and the king of Sodom spake unto Abram that Abram should return the freed prisoners and Abram should keep the plunder from the camp of Chedorloamer,

And Abram was more wily, and Abram refused all plunder and all reward from the king of Sodom lest the people and the

neighbours henceforth deemed the king of Sodom more important,
And Abram's reputation spread.

Genesis 15

And Abram's ego ran rampant once more, and Abram gazed at the stars and dreamed dreams of fame and fortune and numberless descendants,
And then Abram remembered he had no children.

And Abram was hungry and depressed and Abram killed a cow, a goat and a sheep and butchered them,
And the day was hot and the vultured offal stank in the sun,
And Abram dozed in the stench and suffered terrible dreams,
And Abram dreamt his descendants would be slaves, and Abram was disturbed.

And Abram awoke while fire flies buzzed around the stinking carcasses,
And in the dancing lights Abram's ambition sparkled once more,
And the ambition of Abram settled from the great river of Egypt to the mighty Euphrates.

Genesis 16

And Abram knew he must have children, and Abram was frustrated,
And Sarai disgruntled spake unto Abram, Fine, fuck Hagar,
And Abram did so and Hagar, being Egyptian and unrelated to Abram, easily fell pregnant.

And Hagar was happy, and Hagar taunted Sarai by her looks and by her bearing,
And Sarai was not pleased, and Sarai made Hagar do many

menial jobs,

And Sarai bitched about the varicose veins of Hagar and the stretch marks of Hagar,

And Sarai spake unto Abram about the bad behaviour of Hagar, and Sarai moaned much and often to Abram,

And Abram was loyal and a bit wet, and Abram agreed with his wife Sarai, and Sarai had power to treat Hagar as Sarai wished,

And so unpleasant was Sarai, and so hormonal was Hagar, that Hagar left her service and Hagar headed home to Egypt.

But Hagar rested at a waterhole, and Hagar had a think,

And Hagar had no money, and Hagar had no home, and Hagar was with child,

And Hagar plotted revenge through her child, and Hagar was convinced her child would be wild and kickass, and Hagar was convinced her child could cause trouble,

And Hagar turned and Hagar bit the bullet, and Hagar rejoined Abram and Sarai and bore Abram's son Ishmael.

Genesis 17

And Abram was pleased, and Abram strutted,
And Abram decided to rebrand.

And Abram named himself Abraham,
And Abraham once again set his sights on the land of Canaan,
And Abraham wanted a trade mark to mark his clan.

And the mark of Abraham was to be permanent, and the mark of Abraham was to be painful, and the mark of Abraham was to be a commitment and a devotion,

And Abraham ruminated, and Abraham pondered,

And Hagar let Abraham know of a custom in Egypt of male genital mutilation,

And Abraham had heard it made men fertile,
And Abraham still wanted a child from his sister Sarai,
And Abraham set his heart on it.
And Abraham considered Ishmael and felt a little guilty,
But Abraham shrugged, Ishmael would be fine.

And Abraham gathered all his men servants and Abraham summoned Ishmael,
And a witch doctor from Egypt removed their prepuces,
And there was much flailing, and there was much scratching and there was fainting,
And the mark of Abraham was upon his men,
And Abraham was pleased.

Genesis 18

And one day as Abraham was lounging in his tent three strangers approached,
And Abraham rose up and as was the custom Abraham washed their feet and sat them down,
And Abraham offered bread and meat and milk, and they accepted, and they ate.

And the strangers asked after Abraham's wife Sarah (rebranded from Sarai), and Abraham confirmed that Sarah was in her tent, as was the custom,
And the conversation turned to family and Abraham confessed his lack of luck with his wife,
And the three strangers spake unto Abraham thus, Keep trying and it will happen, for they were gentle souls, and encouraging.

And Sarah heard and Sarah giggled,
And one stranger asked why she laughed, and she denied it, and another insisted,

And it was all a little uncomfortable.

So the strangers rose to leave, and Abraham accompanied them some way from his tent,

And as they walked they talked, and the talk turned to Sodom and Gomorrah, wealthy and famous bitumen cities,

And the strangers avowed that they would destroy both Sodom and Gomorrah were they in charge,

For Sodom and Gomorrah were home to rapists and sodomists and sadists.

And the men exchanged tales of Sodom,

And one spoke of the practice of giving beggars gold but refusing to sell them food,

And one related how the girl Palith gave food not gold and as punishment was smeared in honey and hung out for the bees,

And one described how guests' limbs were stretched or chopped to fit beds in guesthouses.

Now Abraham's nephew Lot lived in Sodom, and Abraham felt obliged to defend his blood,

And Abraham agreed a city wholly evil should be destroyed, but cavilled that a city partly good should be left to stand for good men should not suffer for the actions of bad men,

And the strangers grudgingly agreed and headed off to Sodom to party,

For Sodom and Gomorrah were home to hedonists and sensualists and sybarites.

Genesis 19

And only two of the strangers went to Sodom, and it so happened that when they arrived Lot was at the town gates, for Lot's trade was in men and in women,

And Lot eyed them up and down and Lot liked what he saw

and spake unto the strangers, Come stay with me and my virgin daughters,

And the strangers replied No, thank you, we'll see what's what on the street,

And Lot insisted, and Lot promised to throw some food in for free, and the strangers agreed.

And many of the people of the town of Sodom saw Lot take the strangers home,

And the strangers were comely and the people lascivious and the people wanted the strangers and the people besieged Lot's house,

But Lot wanted the strangers also, and Lot went out to speak with the people of Sodom,

And Lot offered the people of Sodom his supposedly virgin daughters in place of the strangers,

And the people of Sodom knew he was lying, for the people of Sodom knew they were married and anyway had been offered them before.

And the people of Sodom surged forward to attack the lying Lot, and the strangers who had listened to the exchange from inside Lot's house pulled Lot back into the house, and threw pepper powder out the doors and windows so as to repel the attacking people of Sodom,

And Lot was grateful.

And the strangers questioned unto Lot thus, Why live in Sodom?

And the strangers spake unto Lot thus, Leave Sodom forthwith for it is decadent and immoral.

Now Lot knew the people of Sodom had marked his card,

And Lot knew now that life in Sodom would be difficult, and Lot felt leaving was a good plan.

Therefore Lot went to his sons-in-law and suggested they

leave, but Lot's fun-loving sons-in-law refused for Sodom was their home.

And Lot took his daughters and his wife and left, and the strangers recommended they go to live the simple life in the mountains, but instead Lot went to visit business contacts in the city of Zoar,

And it came to pass the next day that an earthquake shook the region and the cities of Sodom and Gomorrah were destroyed entirely with no trace remaining.

For Sodom and Gomorrah had been built on saturated soil pocked by pockets of methane and full with bitumen,

And it came to pass that the earthquake caused the saturated soil to liquefy to quicksand and methane gas to be released and bitumen spread all around,

And in the plain view of all around the cities did slide into the sea and the bitumen did burn and the methane did explode, and the cities were utterly destroyed in quake and in fire.

And Lot's wife had tarried, worrying, and was caught in the Dead Sea's burning tidal wave, and Lot's wife was killed in salt and fire.

And Lot and his daughters arrived in Zoar, and the people of Zoar recognised Lot and the daughters of Lot, for Lot and the daughters of Lot were renowned around the area,

And the people of Zoar welcomed not Lot and the daughters of Lot, and bid them leave,

And Lot was penniless, and Lot had no animals, for all was destroyed in Sodom,

And Lot fled the city of Zoar to retreat to the mountains and to a cave.

And Lot and Lot's daughters dwelt in the cave in the mountains, and they lived a simple life and tilled a little land, and kept a few sheep and, lo, even a little vineyard,

And the vines brought forth grapes and the grapes fermented into wine, as for Noah so it was for Lot,

And it came to pass that Lot and Lot's daughters were supping of their wine and partaking of morsels, and talking of the old days in Sodom,

And Lot did miss the screwing and the partying, and Lot did feel pangs of homesickness,

And Lot's daughters did fall asleep,

And Lot was bored and fell to playing with himself and was unsatisfied, and thought unto himself his daughters would better be,

And he and they were shameless and accustomed to depravity and he did wake them and take them and impregnate them.

And it came to pass that the daughter's of Lot bore a child each, and one was named Seed of Father, or Moab, and one was named Benammi,

And from Moab were descended the Moabites, and from Benammi were descended the Ammonites, and in later times the Israelites were unpleasant to these peoples, and blamed it on their ancestral mothers' incest.

Genesis 20

And it came to pass that the fortune of Abraham had waned, and Abraham was in need of shekels and of animals,

And it occurred to Abraham to play his wife/sister card once more,

And Abraham and Sarah travelled to Gerar, and Abimelech king of Gerar took a fancy to Sarah and he took her as his concubine, thinking Sarah was sister to Abraham,

But the truth was out and Abimelech of Gerar did find out that

Sarah was wife not sister,

And Abimelech had heard of Abraham's exploits against Chedorloamer and Abimelech was afraid, and Abimelech returned Sarah to Abraham with many animals and servants,

And Abimelech gave Sarah one thousand shekels and apologised profusely,

And Abraham moved on, rich once more.

Genesis 21

And it came to pass that Sarah fell pregnant, and Sarah gave birth to Isaac, and Abraham mutilated his son as was now his custom, and Isaac grew and was weaned, and Sarah celebrated.

Now Hagar and Sarah were not friends, for Sarah was unpleasant and Hagar had been haughty,

And Sarah wished to dispose of Hagar and her Ishmael,

And it came to pass that Ishmael and Isaac were playing and Ishmael was a little rough and Isaac cried to Sarah,

And Sarah seized the opportunity and complained to Abraham about Hagar and her son.

And Abraham was irked and Abraham did not want to get involved, but Sarah was insistent and Sarah was devilish and Sarah was after all his sister and his wife,

And it was meet and proper that Isaac should be the heir of Abraham as Isaac was his son and nephew,

Therefore Abraham gave Hagar food and water and sent her and Ishmael on their way.

And Hagar and Ishmael walked in the desert and Ishmael hunted and Hagar gathered and in time Hagar found Ishmael a wife from Egypt.

And Abimelech king of Gerar approached Abraham once more for Abraham still dwelt in Abimelech's land,

And Abraham's power and influence was growing,
And Abimelech was afraid of losing springs and wells,
And Abimelech could not oust Abraham through force of
arms but Abimelech could restrain Abraham by treaty,
And Abimelech and Abraham signed a non-aggression pact.

Genesis 22

Now part of that pact involved cultural assimilation,
And strong local custom involved human sacrifice to local
beliefs, in particular sacrifice of eldest children,
And Abimelech was concerned that Isaac lived still,
And Abraham accepted that Isaac must be burned.

So Abraham took Isaac and two servants to the mountains three
days away, and Abraham and Isaac left the servants and climbed
up into the steeps, with Isaac carrying his funeral wood,
And perplexed Isaac asked what they were to burn, and
Abraham muttered something about finding something when
they got to the site, lest Isaac did a runner.

And Abraham found a good spot for the ceremony, and set about
building the pyre,
And Abraham knocked Isaac senseless and bound his legs and
arms and heaved his body onto the pyre,
And Abraham unsheathed his knife and contemplated his
prostrate son, his only son from Sarah.

And as Abraham contemplated, and wondered whether really,
really, this was the right thing to do, a ram struggled in the
undergrowth,
And Abraham could not bear to lose his Isaac,
And Abraham set his mind against the practice: Abimelech
would just have to lump it,
And Abraham knew he could spin the story of the ram beauti-

fully,

And Abraham dragged his son's body from the pyre and replaced it with the ram, and went back to the servants and thence back home to tell the tale of Isaac's miraculous survival and repeat the mantra that his descendants would rule the world.

Genesis 23

And Sarah died, and Abraham was sad of course,

But Abraham, being far from his ancestral home, had nowhere to bury her,

And Abraham spoke to the local landowners and asked to buy a field and a cave,

And Ephron offered him a cave for free but Abraham was too canny for that and insisted that he pay and pay he did,

And Abraham fenced his field and made sure everyone knew he had bought the field for valuable consideration, so Ephron could not renege, for Abraham was old and racist and did not trust his Canaanite neighbours,

And Sarah was buried.

Genesis 24

And Abraham felt it was time Isaac married, and Abraham called his top servant and spake thus, Here, hold my circumcised member as a guarantee of your honesty and promise me Isaac will not marry one of these Canaanites.

And Abraham commanded, Return to my ancestral land and find him a wife.

And the servant queried whether a woman would want to be brought to the land of Canaan to marry a man she had never met, but nevertheless he rather gingerly put his hand under his master's thighs and swore he would do his best.

And the servant packed his bags and headed off to Mesopotamia where Nahor, Abraham's brother lived,

Now Nahor had married his niece Milcah and had eight children, one of whom was Bethuel who had a daughter Rebekah,

And it was to this family that the servant went to find a wife suitably closely related for Abraham's taste.

And the servant arrived in the city in which Nahor lived and went to the well and sat his camels down,

And thought it would be nice to find a kind girl for Isaac, one who would offer to water my camels, for example,

Then Rebekah appeared and the servant ran to see her and asked for water, and Rebekah gave him water and offered some for his camels, and the servant was delighted and gave her some bling,

And it turned out that she was Abraham's great-niece, Isaac's cousin, and she invited the servant to stay.

And the servant met Laban, Rebekah's brother, and announced that he was on a mission from your very rich great-uncle Abraham and he'd like to take Rebekah back to the land of Canaan to marry cousin Isaac, only heir to Abraham,

And Laban and Bethuel couldn't really refuse so they said, OK but can she stay ten days?

And the servant handed over more money but refused the extra time,

And Rebekah was summoned and asked if she was OK with the deal and she couldn't really refuse either,

And off they went: bride purchase complete.

And when they arrived back in the land of Canaan Isaac happened to be out in the field and so Isaac took her by the hand to his dead mother's tent and screwed her,

And it was all very romantic.

Genesis 25

And Abraham took a new wife called Keturah and Keturah was unrelated to Abraham and had no problem conceiving and Keturah bore six children,

But they were of impure blood as far as Abraham was concerned so he sent them away with a sum of money each,

And gave the rest to Isaac.

And eventually Abraham gave up the ghost and Ishmael returned to help Isaac bury Abraham in the cave bought from Ephron,

And it turned out that Ishmael had twelve children with his Egyptian wife and they had spread across the land towards Assyria, each with a town and a castle,

And cousins Isaac and Rebekah had struggled for children.

But in time Rebekah fell pregnant with twins and the foetuses fought and Rebekah was uncomfortable,

And when they were born the second was grasping the first's heel, a sign of things to come,

Jacob and Esau were their names; Esau first out, hairy, ginger and outdoorsy, he was his father's favourite; Jacob second out, was his mother's favourite.

And Jacob and Esau bickered and fought about who was elder,

For though Esau had been first out Jacob had been holding his heel and so perhaps neither was older, or so said Jacob,

And who was eldest mattered greatly, for his was the birthright, the land (despite it being Canaanites'), the leadership, the responsibility for Abraham's eccentric claims,

And one day Esau was hungry and fed up and he caved in: birthright for a bowl of Jacob's stew; it's a deal,

And Esau wasn't bothered, really, he never was ambitious.

Genesis 26

And it came to pass that famine struck once more, and Isaac was forced to leave his land and live in Gerar where a new Abimelech was king,

And Isaac recalled how his father, for safety, used to pretend his wife was his sister,

And Isaac tried the same trick.

But Isaac was not canny as Abraham and Isaac was spotted romping with his 'sister',

And Abimelech demanded answers and Isaac confessed his cowardice and all was fine.

And as Isaac's household grew so did the locals' resentment,

And Isaac was gradually forced away until he reached Beersheba.

And in Beersheba Isaac recalled the dreams of his father, and felt a surge of love,

And Isaac pitched his tent and dug a well and settled down,

And Abimelech visited and signed a non-aggression pact,

And all was well.

And then Esau, ginger Esau, shattered the peace, for Esau was not into in-breeding, nor monogamy, And Esau took himself a pair of Hittite wives; Judith and Bashemath.

And Isaac and Rebekah were appalled.

Genesis 27

And when Isaac was near to death, Esau and his Hittites were excised from the family,

For Isaac sent Esau hunting promising his blessing on his return,

And when he was out Rebekah clothed Jacob in Esau's clothes,

And Rebekah roughed Jacob's smooth skin with goat pelt,

And Rebekah sent Jacob to Isaac to be blessed.

And Jacob did as his mother bade him,
 Now, Isaac was expecting Esau,
 And Isaac knew Esau had gone hunting,
 And Isaac knew Jacob's voice,
 But Isaac nonetheless felt the goat pelt and smelt Esau's clothes and Isaac blessed Jacob.

And Esau arrived home with fresh killed venison and went to his father for his blessing,
 And Isaac broke the news that Jacob had taken the blessing,
 And Esau raged against his cheating lying brother and demanded what exactly Isaac had given him,
 And Isaac admitted he had made Jacob head of the family, with all others to serve him, and had given him the corn and the wine, and, well, pretty much everything...

And Esau begged for some crumb of comfort, and Isaac wondered what was left,
 And Isaac recalled that Esau didn't care much for family history, so he just gave him a standard blessing and promised that he need not always serve Jacob.
 And Esau swore to kill Jacob, once his father was dead.

And so Rebekah thought Jacob should lie low for a while,
 And Rebekah spoke to Isaac thus, These Canaanite women will ruin my life, they already have their claws in Esau and I don't want them getting Jacob.

Genesis 28
And Isaac certainly agreed that Jacob should not marry a Canaanite, He should marry one of us,
 And Jacob was sent to Haran to stay with Rebekah's brother

Laban, to seek a cousin to marry and to avoid fratricide.

And in the meantime Esau got on with his life and added two wives to his harem, and these ones happened to be family, daughters of Ishmael.

And Jacob journeyed to Haran and slept in the desert and dreamt dreams of power and glory, and the conceit of Abraham was in his veins,

And in a flash Jacob understood Abraham's genius,

And Jacob built an altar to his granddad's memory, and reaffirmed the family eccentricity.

Genesis 29

And Jacob arrived at Haran and went to the well, as was customary,

And Jacob chatted to the locals and asked about his family,

And the local lads pointed out Rachel, Jacob's cousin,

Now Jacob knew who Rachel was, for Rebekah of course corresponded with her brother Laban,

And Jacob was smarmy and slippery and knew how to get his way,

And Jacob rushed to the well and opened it up for the pretty little Rachel and gave her a kiss and introduced himself as cousin Jacob, You know – Rebekah's son.

So Rachel took Jacob back to Laban and Laban of course asked him to stay,

And Jacob did so, and Jacob being Jacob with his eyes on the prize helped out on the farm,

And Laban felt a little uncomfortable at Jacob's hard work and asked him what he wanted,

And Jacob said, Rachel. I'll give you seven years' work for Rachel.

And that seemed a fair deal to Laban.

But Rachel was Laban's younger daughter and in Haran it was not done for younger to marry before elder,

And Leah, Laban's elder daughter, was still on the shelf when seven years were up,

And of course Laban gave Jacob Leah first,

And Jacob made a fuss but Laban shrugged, It's unfortunate, but let Leah have her day in the sun and next week you can have Rachel too,

But the offer was not quite what it seemed,

For Jacob had to do another seven years' service for the second.

And after all that fuss, it seems Jacob didn't object to Leah in the slightest,

For in quick succession Leah produced Reuben, Simeon, Levi and Judah,

While Rachel bore none.

Genesis 30

And Rachel, like Sarah before her, knew she needed kids to keep her place,

And Rachel, like Sarah before her, handed over her handmaid, Bilhah,

And Bilhah had Dan and Naphtali,

And Leah took note, and served up her handmaid Zilpah,

And Jacob was happy as a pig in shit.

And Zilpah produced Gad and Asher,

And Rachel was getting desperate, desperately behind in the baby race and losing her looks to boot,

And Rachel in her depression developed something of a habit for the mandrake,

And Leah had a supply of Rachel's Little Helper,

And Leah offered a trade: drugs for sex,

And Rachel surrendered her place in Jacob's bed,

And the mandrake soothed the pain,

But Leah capitalised on her bought sex, producing Issachar, Zebulun and Dinah.

And Jacob did eventually take pity on his poor drug addled erstwhile favourite,

And finally, *finally*, Rachel came to the party and managed little Joseph.

And in time Jacob wished to return to the land of Canaan, and Jacob went to Laban and asked for permission to leave,

And Laban was not keen for Jacob was an excellent shepherd,

And Laban, much as he had fourteen years before, asked Jacob to stay and to name his price,

And Jacob was a bit peeved for he did not want to stay, and he complained that he had worked very bloody hard and now wanted to go home,

And Laban again asked what Jacob wanted.

And Jacob said, No it's fine. Look, we'll divvy up the flocks and I will keep any speckled, spotted or brown offspring and you can keep the others. Deal?

And Laban said, Deal.

So Laban divided the flocks and took all the spotted, speckled and brown ones and kept them separate, three days away.

And Jacob indulged in a little primitive genetic engineering, otherwise known as selective breeding,

And Jacob had a hypothesis that animals conceived near poplar, hazel and chestnut stakes were more likely to be speckled, spotted or brown,

So Jacob made sure the strongest animals conceived near the stakes and the weakest ones were kept away,

And it seemed to work, for Jacob's flocks grew.

Genesis 31

But Laban's sons were not happy, and Laban's sons thought Jacob was thieving,

And Jacob knew his star was waning,

So Jacob called Leah and Rachel to the field and showed them how many animals he had, and explained how he had kept his side of the bargain, and how their father was simply not much of a shepherd, and that he wanted to leave,

And Leah and Rachel pointed out that their father had sold them and pissed away the proceeds, and they were more than happy to leave too.

So Jacob got everything together and, unbeknownst to Jacob, Rachel stole Laban's family idols,

And one day when Laban was visiting distant flocks they left,

But when Laban found out they had gone Laban chased Jacob down,

And Laban pointed out that he should beat Jacob up for this affront, but Jacob was a big bugger and Laban thought the better of it.

But Laban was angry about the family idols and he demanded Jacob return them,

And Jacob denied all knowledge and said he was happy to kill anyone found in possession of them,

So Laban set to searching all through the camp and in time reached Rachel's tent,

Now Rachel had the idols hidden in her seat,

And Rachel was not giving them up,

And Rachel would not stand up, That time of the month, Dad.

Now Jacob really was getting irritated and he demanded to

know what Laban thought he was doing,

And Jacob raged that he had worked twenty years, and Laban had been an arsehole and Laban had docked his wages but Jacob had toiled in the heat of the summer and the frost of the winter and for what? For what??

And Laban calmly pointed out that he was the head of the family and all of this belonged to him: the animals, the women, the children, the servants, everything.

But Laban realised he wasn't going to win this battle, so he proposed a truce.

And Laban and Jacob built a pile of stones to commemorate the truce, and they had a party, and all was well.

Genesis 32

And Jacob continued on his way, pondering the next obstacle in his life: Esau, brother Esau whom he so disgracefully screwed over twenty years ago,

And Jacob took a leaf from the school of opulence diplomacy and dispatched a servant to Esau to boast of his success,

But Esau was already on the road with four hundred men, and that made Jacob nervous.

So Jacob took the precaution to split his party in two, but continued with his shock and awe diplomacy,

And Jacob arranged for three waves of awesomeness to be sent to Esau,

And first went two hundred she-goats, two hundred ewes, twenty billy goats and twenty rams,

And second went thirty milking camels with their foals, forty kine and ten bulls,

And third went twenty she-asses and ten foals.

And Jacob instructed the servant to announce to Esau that

these were a present from Jacob to Esau, a mere trifle of his wealth, sent to indicate his goodwill.

Now Jacob was nervous not only because Esau might still want to kill him,

But Jacob was nervous because his theft was now to become real,

For ever since Jacob stole the blessing he had been in Haran, and he had been Laban's slave, and had not gained any practical benefit from the blessing,

But it would be different in the land of Canaan, Jacob would be head of the family and it was time to make good on the theft.

And Jacob's conscience was understandably uneasy, and an uneasy night ensued, and as he tossed and turned and dreamed and wrestled with his conscience and wrestled with Esau he managed to put his hip joint out,

And Jacob woke and took inspiration from his grandfather's rebrand,

And Jacob became Israel.

For Jacob means 'Cheat' while Israel was something Jacob made up that morning and approximates to He has fought with God, the implication being that he won.

And to reinforce the point, Jacob renamed the place Peniel, or The Face of God.

And Jacob felt a bit braver about seeing Esau.

Genesis 33

And Esau arrived with his four hundred men, and Jacob lined up his women and children in order of seniority (least favourite at the front, then),

And Jacob went to meet Esau, and Esau was chuffed to bits to see his long-lost brother,

For Esau had never really cared about all that birthright blessing business,

And Esau asked what the fuss with all the animals was, and Jacob insisted Esau keep them,

And all was well.

And Jacob (for he remained Jacob, not Israel, once the danger passed) bought some land, built a house, built an altar, and settled down.

Genesis 34

And Leah's daughter Dinah rather enjoyed their new home, and took something of a fancy to the local boys,

And Dinah and local prince Shechem got along famously and Shechem wanted to add Dinah to his harem in a more official capacity,

And Shechem asked his Dad to arrange it.

And when Jacob heard that Shechem had been banging Dinah he was not amused,

And when his sons returned from the fields they heard and were not amused,

But they listened to Shechem's father nevertheless.

And Hamor, Shechem's father, waxed long and lyrical about how much his son loved Dinah,

And about how it would be good for neighbourly relations to have a little inter-marriage,

And how trade would benefit,

And as a sweetener Shechem offered them as much dowry as they liked.

And Jacob and his sons conferred and announced that Shechem would have to become one of them if he were to have Dinah,

And they announced that a full clan merger could take place, with full inter-marrying rights, if Shechem and any others wanting to merge were prepared to suffer Abraham's stamp.

And Shechem and Hamor were delighted, for Jacob and his clan were powerful and an alliance would be excellent news all round,

And Shechem and Hamor returned to their city and told the troops what the plan was, careful to extol the benefits of peace, trade and new women.

And all those who wanted to be part of the revolution met outside the city gates and were circumcised,

And Jacob and the children of Abraham appeared to be all set to abandon generations of institutional racism, generations of obsession about numberless descendants, and generations of religious eccentricity.

But Jacob's second and third born Simeon and Levi had other ideas,

And Simeon and Levi went to the city,

And found Shechem and Hamor and the others still raw and bleeding and in tremendous pain,

And Simeon and Levi killed them,

And Simeon and Levi took their sheep, and their asses, and their goats and their crops,

And Simeon and Levi took their children to be slaves and their wives to be whores,

And Simeon and Levi burnt their houses to the ground.

And Jacob freaked out, What the fuck do you think you're playing at? Do you know what's going to happen now? They will come and do unto me as you have done unto them. We're fucked. Idiots.

Genesis 35

And Jacob decided the best plan, as ever, was to run away,

So Jacob upped sticks and went with his full entourage to Bethel,

And unnerved Jacob started calling himself Israel again,

And Israel made everyone throw away their pagan idols,

And Israel dusted down his revered grandfather's eccentric ways,

And none of the local tribes dared revenge the atrocity.

But times were difficult for Israel,

For his beloved Rachel died giving birth to Benjamin (named Son of my Right Hand, by Israel),

And his firstborn Reuben slept with his concubine Bilhah,

And it was all a bit too much for his old dad Isaac,

And Isaac died aged an improbable 180 and was buried by Israel and Esau.

Genesis 36

And in the meantime outcast Esau was doing fine,

And Esau's many children ruled the lands in which they dwelt,

For they were the children of local women, and were integrated into the local society.

Genesis 37

Now of Israel's eleven children Joseph was Daddy's favourite,

For Joseph was born in Israel's dotage and Joseph was his eyes and ears,

And Israel had a coat made for his little boy, a coat of many colours,

And his brothers, understandably, thought he was a spoilt, sneaking brat.

And Joseph had his great-grandfather's weakness for extravagant dreams,
> And Joseph recounted his dreams to his family,
> And they all thought he was a conceited little twat.

And one day the chance of revenge came to the brothers,
> For Joseph was visiting them in fields far from Israel's protective bubble,
> And Joseph's death was plotted and brothers' alibis planned,
> But Reuben was keen to curry Israel's favour following Bilhah-gate,
> And Reuben intervened, Come off it lads – he's not that bad...
Duff him up and put in a pit for a bit instead.

And they did so duff him up and put him in a pit and as they sat to eat and drink the spectre of Israel's wrath came to them,
> And they resolved to finish the job while Reuben was away,
> But once again Joseph's skin was saved, Judah his guardian this time,
> And Ishmaelite traders paid twenty silver pieces for the poor beaten boy.

And Reuben returned too late,
> And Reuben could never look his father in the eye again,
> And the boys tore Joseph's coloured coat and sent it sprayed with blood to Israel with a sorry tale of lions and hyenas,
> And Israel wept.

Genesis 38
And Leah's son Judah, aping Dinah, took something of a fancy to the local Canaanites,
> And Judah got together with girl next door Shuah,
> And Shuah bore Er, Onan and Shelah.

And Er married Tamar and then died,

And so Onan married Tamar, and then died (some say from excessive onanism),

And Shelah should have married Tamar, for that was the custom,

But Judah was by now a little wary of widow Tamar, and withheld him.

And so frustrated widow Tamar went on the game,
　　And in a twist of fate father-in-law Judah was her john,
　　And wily Tamar took Judah's signet and bracelet in payment.

And in time widow Tamar was found pregnant and threatened with death,
　　But she showed Judah's signet and bracelet,
　　And reminded all that Judah had withheld Tamar,
　　And Judah relented and let her live.
　　And Tamar's twins Pharez (of whose line Jesus Christ would later spring) and Zarah were born.

Genesis 39
And poor Joseph had travelled with the traders,
　　And the traders sold Joseph to Potiphar in Egypt,
　　And Joseph was bright and rose to become overseer,
　　And Joseph was good-looking and wanted by Potiphar's wife,
　　But he wasn't keen,
　　And she was offended,
　　And she set him up and had him sent to jail. Oops.

But in jail talented Joseph again prospered, and received privileges as a trusted inmate.

Genesis 40
And Joseph shared jail with Pharaoh's butler and Pharaoh's

baker,
> And they each dreamed dreams needing interpretation,
> And Joseph thought he'd have a crack.

And it turned out pretty easy, the butler had a lovely dream and the baker had a nightmare,
> And Joseph reasoned that dreaming anticipation is generally accurate,
> So Joseph told the baker he'd be killed and the butler he'd be fine,
> And, lo, both things came to pass.

Genesis 41

And some time later the Pharaoh had recurrent dreams,
> And the butler now in Pharaoh's service recommended Joseph,
> And Joseph was brought and told the dreams,
> And again they seemed pretty clear to Joseph.

So Joseph told the Pharaoh what he thought, One day honey, one day onions; swings and roundabouts; good times and bad times; boom and bust; need I go on, sir? Your dream is a reflection of your nervousness about famine and Egypt's lack of preparedness for such an eventuality.

And Pharaoh was chuffed that someone had finally told him the truth,
> And promoted him to Number 2 ahead of the yes men, which Joseph was chuffed with.
> And called him Zaphnathpaaneah, which Joseph wasn't so chuffed with.

And at the grand old age of thirty Rachel's late effort was second in charge of Egypt, busy busy collecting grain by tax and sons by wife Asenath, pagan daughter of pagan priest Potipherah.

And when famine arrived Zaphnathpaaneah ran the dole.

Genesis 42

And in Canaan also there was famine and Jacob's boys (except Rachel's son Benjamin) went to Egypt for grain,

And Joseph spotted them and remembering his childhood dreams thought he'd mess with their heads a bit.

So Joseph accused them of being spies and Joseph locked them up,

And Joseph noticed Benjamin's absence and guessed the likely explanation,

And Joseph demanded to see Benjamin,

And Joseph took Simeon hostage as collateral,

And the brothers returned to Canaan to collect Benjamin

But doting Israel refused to allow Benjamin out of his sight,

And, lo, Simeon was left to rot in an Egyptian jail.

Genesis 43

But the bought grain ran out and another trip to Egypt loomed,

And Judah made Israel understand, No Benjamin, no food.

And off they went to see Joseph, darling Benjamin in tow.

And Joseph was super-nice and gave them food and Simeon and wined and dined them, Hebrews and Egyptians and Joseph each sitting separately, as was the custom.

Genesis 44

But superniceness did not last long past their release,

For Joseph secreted money and his silver drinking cup in Benjamin's sack.

And soldiers did catch the boys and bring them to Joseph to beg,

And Joseph commanded, He who nicked my cup shall be my

servant, the rest of you can go.

But Judah's neck was on the line for Benjamin,

And Judah translated Benjamin as Son of my Right Hand and told of how great had been the father's love for the mother and still was for the boy,

And Judah in sorrow and in remorse told how the first born of Rachel was no longer with Israel and how old Israel would suffer should Benjamin be taken also.

And Judah sacrificed himself.

Genesis 45

And Joseph could take the pressure no more, and he sent his servants out,

And he confessed that he was Joseph whom they had sold but that he bore them no ill will,

And he spake thus, Look on the bright side - at least now I can help you through the famine, go fetch Dad and all the household and go to live in Goshen; I'll look after you.

And Pharaoh heard what had happened and being keen to keep Joseph he encouraged the resettlement,

And off the brothers went to Canaan to tell Israel the good news.

Genesis 46

And so Israel gathered his clan and decamped to Egypt, invited this time,

And Joseph met them and the shepherds didn't really fit in Egyptian high society.

Genesis 47

And Joseph took some brothers and Israel to meet the Pharaoh,

And Pharaoh gave them Goshen,

And the Hebrews settled in Goshen, shunned by Egypt.

And the famine bit deep and Joseph was busy,
   And as gold became worthless Joseph accepted cattle, horses,
and asses as payment for the Pharaoh's grain,
   And Joseph accepted land as payment for the Pharaoh's grain,
   Until every animal and every acre of Egypt belonged to the
Pharaoh,
   Except of course that which belonged to the priests.

And once Pharaoh owned all the animals and all the land a new
payment paradigm was needed,
   And, behold, securitization was discovered,
   And henceforth Joseph accepted twenty per cent of future
harvests in exchange for seed to sow,
   And recessions have always been good for the rich.

Genesis 48
And when Israel fell ill Joseph brought his sons before him to be
adopted,
   And Israel put his hands on the children's heads, right hand
on Ephraim and left on Manasseh and recited in memory of
Abraham and Isaac,
   And Joseph noted Israel in error had mixed the younger and
the older,
   But Israel insisted he had it right, younger was to rule elder.

Genesis 49
And as Israel was dying he called his sons together for some final
words;
   Reuben: you were my firstborn but your indiscretion with
Bilhah reveals your weakness;
   Simeon and Levi: murderous bastards – your indiscretion was
the start of the rot;

Judah: you, my boy, are a chip off the old block;

Zebulun: I'm not sure I remember you... go and live by the sea;

Issachar: honest and pleasant but lazy and going nowhere;

Dan: sly and silky – you'll do OK;

Gad: learn to fight – you'll be fine;

Asher: you delight in the arts of cooking – indulge yourself;

Naphtali: your nerves have never affected your words;

Joseph: legend and true heir of Abraham, Isaac and Israel; you have survived the slings and arrows of misfortune and you will prosper even until you die;

Benjamin: animal;

Now, all of you, bury me in the cave bought from Ephron,

And, with that, Israel gave up the ghost.

Genesis 50

And Israel was embalmed as was the custom of Egypt and mourned in the custom of Egypt and buried in the cave bought from Ephron.

And without Israel's protection the brothers feared reprisal from Joseph,

But Joseph forgave his brothers, as he said, It all turned out for the best,

And Joseph also died and was embalmed and coffined in Egypt.

Exodus

Exodus 1

And Israel's family did number seventy on settling in Egypt,

And unlike in the land of Canaan there was no friction with the natives,

For Egyptians were tillers of land and Hebrews were keepers of sheep,

And there was no clash, no contest for resources and indeed no interbreeding,

For Egyptians were somewhat snooty about keepers of sheep, Small hands, don't you know,

And all seemed set fair for Abraham's descendants in the lush pastures of Goshen.

But nothing lasts forever and that includes Egyptian dynasties,

And Pharaoh was overthrown and the new Pharaoh owed nothing to Joseph nor to the Hebrews,

And Pharaoh, aware of the doctrine of pre-emptive warfare, waried of the ever expanding Hebrew enclave,

And Pharaoh manacled the Hebrews and enlisted their help with some building projects.

And so the Hebrews screwed and worked and screwed and worked,

And Pharaoh worried and counted and worried some more as the imported population expanded,

And Pharaoh ordered (Hebrew) midwives kill all male (Hebrew) newborns,

But that was a non-starter,

So Pharaoh ordered Egyptians to kill all Hebrew sons,

And that was more realistic.

Exodus 2

And male children became restricted goods in Goshen,

And male children were hidden and raised *in camera*, or abandoned to chance or sold for adoption; anything to keep them living.

And one such was adopted by Pharaoh's daughter and named Moses,

And Moses grew to adulthood mollycoddled, privileged, spoilt and purposeless,

And Moses knew he was a Hebrew but knew he wasn't really,

And he saw a Hebrew slave beaten and he returned a blow in solidarity,

And naively Moses murdered the beater.

And, oh, what an error it was,

For far from feting and praising him, the despising slaves with whom he sympathised recognised and reported him,

And so Moses did as Abraham, Isaac and Israel had done before him; he did a runner.

And Moses did run until he arrived in Midian,

And in Midian he married, procreated and supervised ovine procreation.

Exodus 3

And Moses shepherded and repented at leisure,

And the Hebrew raised as an Egyptian but married to a Midian had ample time alone to ponder,

And Moses knew a little of his family history and knew he was descended of Abraham and Isaac and Jacob and Levi,

And Moses knew of Abraham's ideas on cultural singularity and numberless descendants, ideas sadly fallen into abeyance in the years of slavery,

And a spark flew in Moses' head,

And Moses determined to relight Abraham's fire,

And this time it would burn forever, a bit like those funny oily bush fires that never go out,

And Moses was a man with a plan: pillage Egypt and lead the nation of Israel to freedom and prosperity.

But the plan was more subtle than that: ask Pharaoh to give the slaves three days off for a desert retreat, and THEN don't come back. Cunning.

Exodus 4

And as Moses finessed his plan he realised it was a touch ambitious; ambitious to think the Hebrews would follow a jumped up Pharaoh follower turned slave rights campaigner who had run away at the first sign of trouble, and ambitious to think that Pharaoh would fall for it anyway.

But Moses did a spot of lateral thinking and Moses did imagine a carrot and stick strategy,

And the carrot was to be peace in Egypt and the stick was to be violence,

And Moses recalled a couple of nifty illusions he had learnt from passing circus tricksters,

And Moses reckoned they should do the job.

But again Moses had a sneaking suspicion that his plan was a little lightweight, and indeed that he was a little lightweight,

And Moses knew he needed help and so resolved to persuade brother Aaron, silver-tongued Aaron, to help him.

And so Moses took permission from his father-in-law and headed off across the desert with his wife and his kids,

And poor Moses, wracked with worry about how the plan was going to work, retraced the detail again and again,

And BUGGER! Moses remembered the crucial externality of

the cultural singularity was circumcision.

Now Moses was not circumcised and nor were his children for his adopted mother and his wife both thought it rather barbaric,

But Moses had no choice, or rather his kids had no choice.

And Moses being squeamish asked his wife to do the honours,

And she did,

And she was not amused,

And she threw the severed foreskin at him and stormed back to Midian.

And Moses ploughed on and met up with Aaron and explained the plan, such as it was.

And together they went to see the elders and Aaron did the talking and Moses did his magic tricks,

And the elders thought it worth a try.

Exodus 5

And Moses and Aaron met with Pharaoh and submitted their three day desert retreat request,

And Pharaoh laughed them out of court and doubled the slaves' workload,

As might have been anticipated,

And Moses and Aaron were not exactly flavour of the month.

Exodus 6

But Moses persevered, egged on by forebears' ghosts and belief in cultural singularity,

And Moses insisted he would deliver the Hebrews from their bondage,

And Moses would lead them forth from the burden of slavery,

And they would acclaim his leadership when he delivered them from servitude,

But they didn't believe him.

And Moses and Aaron recalled famous names that rang down the ages,
    Reuben and Simeon, and Levi who lived one hundred and thirty-seven years,
    And Gershon and Kohath and Merari and Libni and Shimi and Amram and Izhar and Hebron and Uzziel,
    All the way to their father Amram who, in family tradition, had wed his blood aunt,
    And their resolve was strengthened.

Exodus 7

And Moses and Aaron returned to Pharaoh and Moses did his magic trick: a snake slithering from his staff,
    But Pharaoh's tricksters matched Moses,
    And Pharaoh sent them packing.

And Moses' plan was failing; neither Hebrew nor Pharaoh had followed it
    And Moses was out of ideas and reduced to muttering dubious threats.
    But then in Santorini a volcano exploded, and in that flash Moses' life changed.

And ash rained over the land and the Nile turned red and foul,
    And fish of the Nile, poisoned and bloated, floated to the sea.

Exodus 8

And frogs escaped the noxious water onto the baking riverbanks,
    And there they perished in the sun,
    And congealing frogs ate no lice nor flies,
    And flies and lice did have dominion over the land.

Exodus 9

And unrestrained lice spread through livestock herds,
  And Egypt's poorly husbanded herds suffered terribly,
  And Egypt's herders fell with boils and blains,
  And as lightning lit the sky volcanic ash rained down as brimstone buckling and crumpling crops.

Exodus 10

And Pharaoh surveyed his flattened harvest, polluted river, extinguished fishery, rotting amphibians, fly-blown carcasses and lice-infested people,
  And as he watched he saw clouds of locusts descend on his remnant of standing crop,
  And then there was darkness.

Exodus 11

And all the while Moses watched,
  And at the junction of each episode Moses claimed the credit,
  And at each junction Moses demanded that Pharaoh release the Israelites,
  And each time Pharaoh refused, or acceded and then changed his mind
  And Moses, an opportunist like his old man Abraham, knew this was the time to go,
  For the carefully kept Israelite flocks were more or less intact,
  And the Israelite people had suffered far less by the volcano,
  And the Egyptians were almost willing to believe Moses had caused it all, even though stuff like this had happened before.

And Moses instructed the Israelites to thieve all they could from their Egyptian neighbours and prepare to leave.

Exodus 12

But one final persuasive blow had to be struck; Pharaoh had to be convinced that the Israelites leaving was a Good Thing,

Now Moses knew the power of theatre and of ritual, and also of terror,

And Moses recalled Pharaoh's attempts to kill all male Hebrew children,

And Moses hatched a plan.

And Moses instructed all the Israelites to take a perfect one year old male lamb,

And the lamb was to be taken into the household and treated as part of the family,

And the lamb was to be slaughtered in full assembly on the fourth day.

And Moses instructed his people to splash blood on the side posts and the upper post of their front door,

And then to roast the lamb's head, legs and offal and eat it all: eat it quickly and eat it with bitter herbs, and burn any leftovers,

And then eat only unleavened bread for seven days, with assembly on the first day and on the last,

And no foreigners, or at least no uncircumcised foreigners, were permitted to join the party.

And this rite was to be repeated every year henceforth so as to keep alive the memory of the Great Escape,

For Moses knew the night of the bloody door posts would be their last night in Egypt,

For Moses knew that killers would be loose executing every firstborn child of man or beast found behind an unmarked door.

And on the appointed night at the appointed hour the special force went about its business,

And Pharaoh was woken from his royal slumber and informed of the atrocity,

And Pharaoh summoned Moses and Aaron and told them to leave,

And horrified Egyptians hurried six hundred thousand Israelites to the exit,

And the six hundred thousand carried dough for bread they had not time to leaven,

And they carried gold and silver and jewels stolen from the Egyptians,

And they drove their flocks and their herds,

And non-Israelites were part of the crowd too, whether as slaves or volunteers is not recorded,

And Egypt was glad to see the back of the four hundred and thirty year Israelite enclave,

For terror had gained its victory.

Exodus 13

And it was decreed that the ritual of the lamb and the unleavened bread was to be repeated each year in remembrance of the death of the first-born in every Egyptian household,

And in remembrance of the price of freedom,

But not until they were settled in the lands of the Canaanites and the Hittites and the Amorites and the Hivites and the Jebusites,

For there were more pressing issues to deal with, such as how to complete the escape.

Now Moses knew his flock were not fighters,

And on the most direct route to the Canaanites' land of milk and honey lived the warrior Philistines,

And the Philistines would be keen to nick the gold, silver, jewels, cattle, sheep and goats the Israelites had nicked from Egypt,

So that route was best avoided and instead they headed another more roundabout route, lugging old Joseph's bones with them,

And Moses led from the front with smoke signals by day and a bonfire by night.

Exodus 14

And almost immediately Egypt recovered its senses,

And Pharaoh missed his workforce, for they had been a diligent workforce,

And Pharaoh resolved to round them up and put them back to work,

And he fired up his chariot squadron and his horsemen and hunted the Hebrews down, catching up with them near the canal that ran from Lake Timsah to the Mediterranean,

And as Pharaoh encircled the runaways a mighty whinge went up,

And whining filled the air as Moses was inundated with complaints and told-you-sos,

And the wannabe nation would rather be back making bricks for the Pharaoh than facing an ignominious death at the hands of the charioteers,

But Moses said, Hang on, lads, I've got an idea.

For seeing the nearest section of the canal almost dry, Moses urged his throng across it,

And when the chariots and horses followed they did struggle in the mud,

And as they thrashed and floundered Moses kicked chunks of the canal walls and walls of water broke forth,

And harnessed horses whinnied water at the last,

And armoured riders gurgled for their mothers,

And once more was Moses flavour of the month.

Exodus 15

And as they saw the enemy destroyed the Israelites began their partying,

And Miriam and her girlfriends got their timbrels out and danced the night through,

And there was much rejoicing and crowing,

And a victory song was penned, and sung.

But Moses' honeymoon didn't last long for unsurprisingly the six hundred thousand strong party in the desert soon ran out of water,

And again there was whining from the camp,

And whinging ungrateful elements and politicking elements and wannabe leaders fomented unrest,

But Moses ordered a well dug at Marah,

And despite the water being bitter from salt and nitre it was at least drinkable.

And Elim was the next resting place,

And Elim had twelve wells; conveniently one for each tribe,

And it was good.

Exodus 16

And as the party traipsed further into the desert food became scarce and again the whines were heard from the camp, and the whinging grew ever stronger, and the ungrateful elements and the politicking elements and the wannabe leaders fomented unrest,

And ingrates muttered that being a fat slave was preferable to being a starving freeman,

But Moses told them, Get a grip and do a little foraging. Look we have mushrooms and insects and their honeydew, and we have lichens and tamarisk sap and of course there are quails. We will not starve if we show a little ingenuity.

And Moses was right again, for there were plenty of bits of food to gather,

And the Israelites gathered and gathered enough for days but found that unprepared gatherings went maggoty overnight,

And so as to avoid work on their rest day the Israelites cooked their rest day's food the day before, and the cooked food kept clean overnight.

And Moses ordered that a pot of some of the more delicious mushrooms they found should be kept for posterity.

Exodus 17

And the party moved on from Sin to Rephidim, digging wells as they went,

But the Israelites were now in Amalek territory,

And the Amaleks were keen to keep the foragers off their land, a plague of locusts would have been preferable,

And the Amaleks attacked.

And Joshua and his squad were sent by Moses,

And the Amaleks were cut to pieces,

And a grateful Moses did build a monument to celebrate Hebrew military prowess,

For Moses did recognise that war would be a constant feature in the future of a fledgling landless nation.

Exodus 18

And it came to pass that Moses' feats and the flight of the Hebrews became known around the world,

And Moses' father-in-law Jethro heard and came unto Moses to congratulate and to weigh up future prospects,

And Jethro spake thus, I always knew you had it in you.

And Moses introduced Jethro to his friends and advisors,

And Moses invited Jethro to sit in on his ruling council,

And unto Moses came all the people with their trifling

problems,

    And Moses did give judgments.

And Jethro was bemused, Surely you have people who can deal with this? You'll wear yourself out, my boy. This is no sort of work for a great leader.

    And Moses listened and learned and realized his position,

    And Moses appointed judges and superjudges and underjudges,

    And Jethro, his work as father-in-law done and not rating the future prospects highly, did head home to Midian.

Exodus 19

And the Hebrews moved once more and came unto Sinai and camped under the hill,

    And Moses now freed from his role as judge and arbitrator had time to ponder,

    And in his reverie he fretted that the people no longer needed him,

    And Moses called his people together and together they reaffirmed their allegiance to the man who had brought them out of Egypt,

    And Moses was satisfied.

And in his reverie he fretted that the Hebrews would stray from Abraham's singular vision,

    And he contemplated the whinging and the whining and the behaviour of Reuben and Levi and Simeon,

    And he pondered Noah's ancient laws,

    And he dismissed the Egyptians' brutal laws,

    But a little discipline and clarity of purpose for the group would be a Good Thing,

    For his judges judged inconsistently and the rule of law was in its infancy.

And Moses' theatrical leanings came to the fore,

And Moses made a plan.

And Moses envisioned thunder and lightning and a sonorous voiceover,

And a high impact audiovisual spectacular was the order of the day,

And ritual too – ritual is important,

And what better ritual for signifying importance than sexual abstinence?

And control – illusionism needs control.

And Moses descended from his hilltop lair,

And Moses did announce that a new order was to be instigated,

And the people should be ready to receive the Law,

And the people were to wash their clothes and repeat verses in suitably solemn fashion,

And no sex please for three days.

And in three days there would be thunder and lightning and smoke and mirrors,

And all stand back from the mountain please, else you get an arrow in the neck.

And Moses returned to the mountain to finalise his preparations,

And Moses found some of the bushes that burn, and collected great stocks of smoky burning material,

And on the third day Moses did light the fires and smoke did rise all around the hill,

And the six hundred thousand intrigued spectators did keep their distance.

And trumpets sounded and Moses asked for quiet.

Exodus 20

And a voice rang out from within the smoke:

We are the Hebrew nation, which has come out of the land of Egypt, out of the house of bondage, we are of pure blood and these are the rules by which we shall live.

We shall not corrupt our purity nor bow down nor serve any other master; for we are the Hebrew nation.

We shall visit the iniquity of them that stray from our identity upon their children unto the third and fourth generation. But those that remain within the bosom of the nation shall know our mercy.

We shall not take the name of our nation in vain, and we shall not hold him guiltless that doth take our name in vain.

We shall honour our fathers and our mothers, and our days shall belong upon the land which the nation shall grant unto us.

We shall take every seventh day for rest. Six days we shall labour, but the seventh day is the day of rest: in it no man may force labour, nor shall we force labour on our son, nor our daughter, nor our manservant, nor our maidservant, nor our cattle, nor any stranger that is within our gates.

We shall not kill.
  We shall not commit adultery.
  We shall not steal.
  We shall not bear false witness against our neighbour, nor shall we covet our neighbour's house, nor our neighbour's wife, nor his manservant, his maidservant, his ox, his ass, nor any thing that is our neighbour's.

And with that the voice ceased and Moses did mount up into the smoke saying he must hammer out the fine details of the laws and would be back soon.

And Moses returned to his lair, now a little smoky, and took his pen and paper and wrote and wrote,

And Moses sketched out rules for every eventuality he could conceive:

And Moses' first priority was maintenance of Abraham's singular identity,

But Moses did know he was powerless to halt the old ways of animal sacrifice,

And so Moses did modify the rules a little for the modern age:

The people shall not make any graven image, or any likeness of anything that is in the earth or that is in the water under the earth for that is the way of the Egyptians and not of our nation; should they wish to demonstrate gratitude for their lot they should burn animals on non-hewn stone platforms,

No other way was to be permitted.

Exodus 21

And Moses moved to the minutiae: duration and governance of slave terms, women's rights, punishment of criminals and their animals, rules of courtesy, money lending and when to party.

If you do as you are told and we all stick together then all will be well – we will destroy our enemies and wreck their temples and take their lands,

But not all at once – if we destroy them in one go then the infrastructure will be ruined and we will not survive; no, we must take over gradually and by weight of numbers not by brute force.

And given time we will take from the Red Sea to the Sea of the Philistines, and from the desert to the river and the Amorites and

Hittites and Perizzites and Canaanites and Hivites and Jebusites will be destroyed. Mwhaahaahahahahahaaa…

Exodus 24

And on completion of the tome Moses did return to the people and did pile some unhewn stones together with twelve pillars to represent the twelve children of Israel,

And young men killed bullocks and burnt them and Moses sprinkled blood,

And Moses read his new rules out,

And the people acclaimed and affirmed their obedience,

And it was good.

And Moses gathered his advisors for a celebratory banquet,

And at the banquet there was merriment and back slapping for all seemed set fair,

Except for the rather low rent altar Moses had piled together,

And Moses had some more ideas, and off he wandered to flesh them out,

And Moses was gone for forty days and forty nights.

Exodus 25

And Moses reconsidered the rules concerning unhewn stone altars,

And Moses thought they were perhaps lacking in imagination,

And a focal point was needed for people's troubles and desires,

And a sanctuary seemed a good idea,

With an ark inside it.

And now Moses' pent up artistic urge came boiling forth,

And Moses dreamed of gold and silver and brass fittings,

And blue and purple and scarlet linen and goat's hair,

And rams' skins dyed red and badgers' skins and shittim wood,

Oooh… and oil and spices and sweet incense and onyx stones and and and…

And Moses set to sketching rings and staves and cherubims for the ark,

And mercy seats and gold overlays and gold crowns and gold spoons and dishes and candlesticks shaped like almonds with knob and flower motifs,

And lamps and tongs and snuffdishes…

Gosh – how stylish it will all be.

Exodus 26

And Moses dreamed of a tabernacle with curtains of fine twined linen in blue and purple and scarlet with loops of blue and taches of gold,

And curtains of goats' hair,

And a covering of rams skins dyed red and badgers' skins too,

And silver sockets and shittim boards with gold overlay,

And a veil of linen with cherubims to keep the ark behind.

Exodus 27

And the altar – the piéce de resistance,

Shittim wood with horns at the corners,

With brass pans and shovels and basins and fleshhooks and a brass grate and, well, all utensils in brass,

And a courtyard around the tabernacle made from curtains of fine twined linen,

And Aaron and his sons would burn lamps at the tabernacle at all times, fuelled by olive oil brought by the people.

Exodus 28

For Aaron was to be in charge of the tabernacle and the ark,

So Aaron should be suitably attired,

A breastplate, an ephod, a robe, an embroidered coat, a mitre and a girdle should do nicely,

And the ephod of gold and blue and purple and scarlet and fine twined linen, and the girdle made of the same,

And the names of the children of Israel engraved on onyx stones,

And the onyx set in gold and set on the shoulders of the ephod.

And the breastplate also of gold and blue and purple and scarlet and fine twined linen,

And in it set sardius and topaz and a carbuncle,

And a row of emerald, sapphire and diamond,

And then ligure, agate and amethyst,

Lastly beryl, onyx and jasper,

All set in gold.

And there will be gold rings and chains and blue lace embroidered with golden bells and pomegranates too,

And Aaron will look smashing.

And a hat too, a gold plate on a blue lace mitre. Marvellous.

And a uniform for his boys too: linen would be nice.

Exodus 29

And next Moses planned the animal burning, and let no man say he got a little carried away.

So take one bullock and two rams (healthy, not deformed ones) with unleavened cakes and wafers,

And bring them to the tabernacle and wash the animals,

Get Aaron kitted up and anoint him with oil, get the boys kitted up too,

And bring a bullock to the tabernacle door and kill in full view of all,

And dip your finger in the blood and trace it down the horns on the corners of the altar,

The remainder of the blood tip away.

Take the fat around the innards, the liver and the kidneys and burn them on the altar,

Take the flesh, skin and dung and burn them outside.

Take a ram and while the boys hold it Aaron will kill it and spray its blood on the altar,

Dress it, wash it and burn it on the altar.

Take the other ram and kill it in the same way, and take some blood and trace it onto Aaron's right ear, and the boys' right ears, and their right thumbs and their right big toes,

And spray some more onto the altar,

And take some oil and some blood from the altar and flick it all over Aaron.

And take the fat around the innards, the rump, the liver, the kidneys and the right shoulder, some bread and a wafer and wave it around in the air,

And then burn them on the altar.

And take the breast of the ram and wave it around in the air and put it aside for Aaron to eat later along with the second shoulder,

And seethe the remainder of the ram and Aaron and his boys will eat it at the door of the tabernacle, any leftovers are to be burnt.

We'll do a bullock a day for a week and then stick with a lamb in the morning and evening daily.

Exodus 30

And it crossed Moses' mind that the altar and indeed the tabernacle might become a little pungent over time,

And Moses designed a darling little incense altar too, incense to be burnt each and every day,

And Moses had a wash station installed at the entrance of the tabernacle for Aaron and his boys to clean the sand off their feet and the grime from their hands,

And the anointing oil was to be perfumed too,

All paid for by a half-shekel poll tax.

Exodus 31

And Bezaleel and Aholiab were known to be the most talented craftsmen in the party, and were earmarked for the job,

And Moses noted again the importance of the labour laws and that even Bezaleel and Aholiab should not work on the seventh day,

And chuffed with his new designs, Moses headed back to the main party with his new rules engraved on stone.

Exodus 32

Now Aaron was in charge while Moses was up the hill,

And in Aaron's charge the whining and the whinging grew within the camp and the naysayers and the wannabes grew voluble,

And they did rake over Moses' past as an Egyptian-raised dilettante,

And they did ponder the meaning of Moses' strange and unexpected exit from the banquet,

And it was said he was not returning and it was said his Midianite family were too dear to him,

And they did lean on Aaron to give the people succour.

Now Aaron had never really bought into the no-graven-images rule,

Nor indeed the whole cultural singularity project,

And Aaron commandeered all the golden earrings of the people,

And Aaron constructed a gorgeous golden calf and placed it on an altar,
And the people loved it and sacrifices were burnt and offerings made,
And the people unloosed from Moses' Spartan regime of foraged food and puritan meditation,
And the people partied.

As Moses approached the partying Hebrews something was clearly amiss – too much jollity and too many smiling faces,
And it dawned on him what the little buggers were up to,
And he realized his authority had been compromised,
And he swore to himself he would execute every last motherfucking one of them,
But then he recalled all the graft that had got them there,
And he didn't want to let Abraham and Isaac and Israel down,
And the red mist parted from his sight.

And Joshua rushed to Moses and blamed the noise on a fight,
And Moses corrected him grimly, It is singing.

And Moses rounded the final corner and beheld the golden calf, the writhing bodies, the excess and the heat,
And in Moses' rage the engraved tablets went smashing,
And the calf was hurled to the fire and burned,
And Moses took the burned calf and ground it down,
And as a dog is made to eat its own misplaced mess, the Israelites were made to drink their ground folly.

And Aaron quivering before Moses' rage explained, We thought you'd left us... We thought you weren't coming back... We needed distraction from this shitty desert.

And Moses saw the people really had gone to seed,

And the singing and the dancing demonstrated total breakdown in his absence,

The freed slaves now unchecked had lapsed into savagery.

And Moses summoned his faithful Levite death squad and sent it forth,

And discipline was restored by the blade of the sword and the ferocity of the beatings,

And three thousand revellers lost their lives,

And the rotting carcasses spread sickness in the camp

And Moses' iron fist prevailed.

Exodus 33

And Moses knew the time had come to move to Canaan and to eject the peoples there,

And the Hebrews did mourn Moses' decision, for desert life was peaceful,

And Moses ordered all to put away their decoratives and prepare for hardship,

And Moses went in to his tent shrouded in incense to meditate and make some plans.

Exodus 34

And early morning Moses went up unto the hill,

And new tablets of stone were carved,

And Moses resolved again to destroy the Amorites and the Canaanites, the Hittites and the Perizzites, the Hivites and the Jebusites,

And Moses determined to maintain the purity of his force,

And Moses blamed the calf incident not on dear brother Aaron but on the foreigners in their midst,

And henceforth no foreign gods would be permitted,

And no foreign women tolerated,

And total war would be waged on the olive groves and the

altars and the images of the enemy.

And the Great Escape be remembered always,
    And every male firstling animal and human was to be burnt or redeemed,
    And the seventh day would be for rest,
    And the people would party three times a year: the Great Escape, the sowing of the crops and the harvest.

And Moses pondered on his people's attachment to superstition,
    And ever the pragmatist, Moses turned it to his gain
    And Moses caught a ram and fashioned himself a horned headpiece,
    And he did don it when he came down from the hill.

And the headpiece scared the Hebrews,
    And Moses summoned them and passed on the tablets,
    And Moses covered his head with a veil,
    And henceforth when Moses did enter his tent he exited not without his horned headpiece.

Exodus 35

And Moses raised a charity appeal for stuff to build the tabernacle and the altar and the clothes,
    And the terrified people poured forth their bracelets and earrings and rings and tablets of gold,
    And men brought blue and purple and scarlet linen and goat's hair and red skins of rams and skins of badgers,
    And shittim wood piled up, and silver and brass stacked together,
    And women spun goat's hair,
    And rich kids brought onyx and spice and oil and incense.

And Bezaleel and Aholiab were appointed as master builders.

Exodus 36

And Bezaleel and Aholiab surveyed the piles of wood and stacks of metal and rolls of cloths and skins,

And they said, What we meant to do wiv all that? 's enuff to build a bloomin' castle.

And Moses did cancel the charity appeal,

And the pair did set to work to make the tabernacle to Moses' specifications.

Exodus 37

And Bezaleel did make the ark to Moses' specifications.

Exodus 38

And Bezaleel did make the altar to Moses' specifications,

And Bezaleel did use twenty nine talents of gold (that is 994 kilograms).

And one hundred talents of silver (that is 3422 kilograms),

And seventy talents of brass (that is 2408 kilograms),

And the thing weighed in around 7 tonnes, once cloth and skin and wood was added in.

Exodus 39

And the pair did make Aaron's clothes to Moses' specifications,

And the ephod was a lovely thing of gold, blue, purple and scarlet with gold thread and onyx stones and bells and pomegranates,

And they brought it before Moses and Moses near fainted with delight.

Exodus 40

And Moses did instruct Aaron in how he wished the new kit to be used,

And flames were lit all around and the tabernacle was kept brightly lit by night and shrouded in smoke by day.

Leviticus

Leviticus 1

And Moses did move on to the next phase of his nation building,
    For the Hebrews now had Rules and Regulations,
    And the Hebrews had a community focal point,
    But the Hebrews still lacked moral guidance and enforcement;
ethics and principles and sanctions.

And another consideration weighed on Moses: Aaron.
    Now Moses had no children, or at least only Midianite
children,
    But unto Aaron was born four boys,
    And Aaron had been instrumental in the Great Escape,
    And post-Escape Aaron's oratory had been exemplary and
binding,
    And we'll gloss over the calf incident.

And Moses offered Aaron and his boys to be keepers of the tabernacle, guardians of the ark, exclusive users of the altar,
    With a perpetual sinecure of meat and flour paid as tax on
children and animals born and as fines levied,
    And Aaron accepted gleefully.

Leviticus 2-7 in appendix

Leviticus 8

And the day dawned for Aaron's appointment as Moral Tax
Collector in Chief,
    And a bullock, two rams and a basket of unleavened bread
were brought,
    And Aarons' and his sons' new threads were gathered
together,

And the entire party of six hundred thousand gathered at the door of the tabernacle,

And Moses washed Aaron and his sons with water,

And Moses dressed Aaron in his coat and girdle and ephod,

And Moses strapped Aaron into his breastplate with representations of Doctrine and of Truth,

And Moses placed Aaron's mitre upon his head,

And took the oil and sprayed it around the tabernacle and the altar and Aaron's head.

And Moses dressed Aaron's sons in coats and girdles and bonnets,

And the bullock was brought and Aaron and the boys held it and Moses slit its throat,

And Moses dipped his finger in the blood and painted it on the horns around the altar,

And Moses took the fat and the kidneys and the liver and burnt them on the altar,

And Moses took the remainder of the bullock and incinerated it outside the camp.

And the ram was brought and again Aaron and the boys held it and Moses slit its throat,

And Moses sprayed the blood around the altar,

And Moses dressed the ram and burnt the head and the fat,

And Moses washed the innards and the legs and then burnt it all on the altar.

And the final ram was brought and Aaron and the boys held it and Moses slit its throat,

And Moses dipped his finger in the blood and painted it on the right ear of Aaron and the right thumb of Aaron and the right big toe of Aaron,

And Moses did the same to the sons of Aaron.

And Moses took the fat, the rump, the fat of the innards, the kidneys, the liver, the right shoulder, some unleavened bread and gave them to Aaron,
Aaron promptly gave them back,
And Moses burnt them.

And Moses took some blood mixed with oil and flicked it at Aaron,
And Moses said, Eat what you like of the leftovers and burn what you leave over,
Do not leave the tabernacle for seven days.

And that was that; Aaron was ensconced in one of the cushiest jobs in history.

Leviticus 9

And silver-tongued Aaron thought a party was in order,
And Moses was aware of his people's proclivity for partying,
And on the eighth day Moses did order the killing of a calf and a ram and a goat with great ceremony,
And the animals were burnt as Moses had decreed,
And the people did watch and shout and fall on their faces, drunk and happy.

Leviticus 10

And Aaron's boys Nadab and Abihu did get a little carried away,
And Nadab and Abihu had raided Aaron's booze cupboard,
And Nadab and Abihu did throw a little extra something onto the fire,
And the fire did burn strongly,
And Nadab and Abihu were burned alive.
And their cousins Mishael and Elzaphan did carry their bodies out.

And not for the first time the majority were punished because a minority had broken ranks,

For Moses banned booze for Aaron and his boys.

Leviticus 11

Now Moses was content with the progress he was making,

For Moses now had judges and laws and ceremony and gaiety,

But still some decorum was missing, a little je ne sais quoi,

And Moses did realise his people's diet was a little, shall we say, carefree,

And people did eat more or less anything,

And people did get sick,

And Moses' ideal state had no sickness,

And Moses' ideal state ate no exotica.

And Moses noted that camels and coneys and hares and pigs were all for one reason or another not suitable to eat,

And Moses noted that each of them either did not chew the cud or did not have a cloven hoof,

And Moses announced that henceforth only animals that chewed the cud and had cloven hooves could be eaten by his people,

And while many bemoaned the loss of ham and bacon, many were happy to be shot of camel hump.

And prawns and shellfish were delicious but only at the seaside,

Ditto dolphin fat,

And dolphins had no scales, and shellfish had no fins,

And Moses decreed; only fish with scales and fins were to be served á table.

And Moses did consider birds,

But Moses could not put his finger on a rule, however

tenuous, to exclude exotica from the range of edible birds.
　So Moses banned eating of eagles (tough),
　And of ossifrages (rotten bone marrow scavengers),
　And of ospreys (cannibals),
　And of vultures and kites (soldier scavengers),
　And of ravens (utterly omnivorous),
　And of owls (tough),
　And of night hawks (ostriches again),
　And of cuckows (actually seagulls; see cormorants),
　And of cormorants (water raven),
　And of great owls (see eagles),
　And of swans (actually an owl),
　And of pelicans (eat shellfish in their shells, vomit them up
and pick out the meat from the opened shell),
　And of gier eagles (feed their young on blood),
　And of storks (rather pretty),
　And of herons (useful for hunting),
　And of lapwings (nest in dung),
　And of bats, for Moses was rather freaked out by bats.

And Moses did ban flying insects (cockroaches, moths and
mosquitoes; not missing out on much),
　But allowed the delicious, plentiful and nutritious locust,
　Ditto bald locusts, grasshoppers and beetles.

And dogs and cats and bears have paws,
　And weasels and mice and tortoises and ferret and
chameleons and lizards and snails and moles were all deemed a
little exotic,
　And exotica causes disease,
　And so anything edible touched by anything exotic must be
thrown away,
　Except, obviously, sowing seed for that will not be eaten
directly.

And anything used for cooking touched by any of these must be thrown away or cleaned.

And all creepers (snakes and the like) should be avoided.

Leviticus 12

And while on hygiene Moses moved from food to childbirth,
   And post-partum women were corralled for a month or so,
   Having paid Aaron a lamb and a pigeon per birth.

Leviticus 13

And from childbirth to sickness,
   And anyone with a lesion looking like leprosy must report to Aaron,
   And Aaron shall keep him under observation in seven day periods,
   And diagnose leprosy or health.

And Moses did decree that it was OK to be bald,
   But not if there is a white reddish sore for that is a sure sign of leprosy,
   And any man declared leprous shall have his clothes removed and hat taken from him,
   And he shall grow a moustache,
   And everyone shall point and shout and laugh at the moustache,
   And all the world shall know he is leprous,
   And he shall be forced out of the camp to suffer by himself.

And the clothes of the leper shall be examined and kept under observation,
   And if the leprosy is in the clothes they shall be burnt,
   And if the leprosy is not in the clothes they may be washed and washed then worn again.

Leviticus 14

And a leper who has healed shall be examined by Aaron and his boys,

And the price of readmission to the camp shall be two birds; one to be killed and one set free,

And the ex-leper shall wash himself and shave his head,

And the ex-leper shall hang around post-wash for seven days,

And then the ex-leper shall pay two male lambs, one female lamb, three tenth deals of fine flour and one log of oil to Aaron and his boys,

Or one lamb and two turtledoves for pauper lepers,

And blood and oil shall be spread in all the usual places,

And the right ear and right thumb and right toe shall be oiled and bloodied.

And Aaron and his boys shall always be in charge of this nice little earner,

And in time when Canaan is conquered Aaron and his boys will certificate houses as free from or suffering from leprosy,

And leprous houses shall be cleaned or destroyed if the cleaning is ineffective,

And if cleaned then the price for readmission is two birds; one to be killed and one set free.

Leviticus 15

And from skin sickness to bodily discharge sicknesses, gonorrhoea and diarrhoea,

And Moses decreed that everything touched by a gonorr/diarrhoeal was unclean and must be washed, including beds, chairs, people, saddles,

And anything that touched anything that had been touched must be washed,

And any man healed of his bodily fluid discharge must wash seven days until he is properly clean,

And on the eighth day he must pay Aaron and his boys two turtledoves.

And not content with sickness discharge, Moses looked to wipe away all discharge,

And drafted rules on washing semen stains and periods,

For semen must be washed from wherever it lands

And periods were to be suffered out of camp,

And goner/diarrhoeals too,

And the price of readmission to camp is two turtledoves.

Leviticus 16

Now Aaron wished to commemorate his sons burnt in the Special Brew incident,

And Aaron took a bullock, a ram and two goats,

And killed and burned all bar one goat,

And released the survivor unto the wilderness to roam immemorial.

And it was decreed that on the tenth day of the seventh month no work should be done,

And it shall be a rest day to recall the deaths of Aaron's sons, and all others who die by misadventure.

Leviticus 17

Now it was true that Aaron and his boys exacted payments for animal killings, for disease management and for women's periods,

And one would have thought that would be enough,

But one would be wrong,

For Moses now decreed that ALL edible animals killed by a Hebrew were to be brought unto Aaron and the boys and tax paid,

And Aaron shall sprinkle some blood about and burn some

fat to earn his meat,

And in this way no Hebrew shall make sacrifices to pagan gods in the fields,

And central control shall be maintained.

And the penalty for not paying tax to Aaron and the boys was ostracism,

And a penalty must be paid should the animal have no blood for Aaron to sprinkle,

For fresh blood must not be drunk, but given to Aaron and his boys.

Leviticus 18

And Moses felt secure with his hygiene rules,

And all was in order.

And Moses moved on to other Rules for Civilisation,

And Moses decreed that interfamilial sex was a no-no,

For too long this sort of thing had gone on unchecked,

And now it had to stop.

And sex with your mother, your mother-in-law, your sister, sister-in-law, granddaughter, auntie, uncle's wife, daughter-in-law, sister-in-law were all forbidden,

Sex with two generations of the same family, or indeed three, was on the naughty list,

Nor was your wife's sister a suitable target,

Sex with women on the blob: banned,

Sex with your neighbour's wife: proscribed,

Sending your semen to Molech: disallowed,

Man on man: an abomination and forbidden,

Bestiality: confused and most definitely illegitimate, and that goes for men and for women.

And all these practices were common in the land of the Amorites and the Canaanites, the Hittites and the Perizzites, the Hivites and the Jebusites,

But the Hebrew nation shall not practice them, nor any man who visits with us,

For they are abominations.

Leviticus 19

And Moses again recapped the basic Rules of the Hebrews:

No superstition, honour your mother and father, rest on every seventh day, don't leave uneaten food until it goes off,

When you harvest, leave some scraps for the poor,

Don't steal, defraud nor lie,

Pay wages promptly,

Don't curse the deaf nor trip the blind,

Don't raise the poor on a pedestal, nor fawn over the rich,

Don't gossip, but don't withhold truth,

Don't hold grudges, talk them over,

And love thy neighbour as thyself.

Don't interbreed species of animals, nor mix seeds in a field, nor cloths in a fabric,

Sex with a slave girl costs one ram to Aaron and the boys,

And don't eat fruit from trees under five,

Don't eat bloody meat, nor practice witchcraft,

Let your curly hair grow long,

No tattoos and no self-mutilation,

No pimping out your daughter,

Don't hang out with witches,

Honour old people,

Be nice to strangers,

Oh, and don't use scam weights.

Leviticus 20

And no child sacrifice, on penalty of death by stoning,
And any man covering up child sacrifice shall be ostracised.

And those who consort with witches shall be ostracised.
And those who curse their parents shall be killed,
And those that commit adultery shall be killed,
And mothers-in-law and daughters-in-law and their shaggers shall be killed,
And practising gays shall be killed,
And multigenerational shaggers shall be burnt,
And bestialists shall be killed, the animal too,
But for shagging your sister, half-sister ('doing an Abraham', as it was known) or a woman on the blob then ostracism is punishment enough,
Unspecified punishment for shagging your aunt or uncle's wife,
Doomed to childlessness for shagging your sister-in-law.

And if we do all these things and eat the right food and keep ourselves morally pure we shall inherit the earth.

Leviticus 21

And so far so good,
And the irregular and the exotic was being erased,
And Moses wanted his enforcers to practice more what they preached,
And Moses set some rules for Aaron and his boys,
And they were not to touch dead bodies save those of close family,
And they were not to self-mutilate nor cut their beards nor their hair,
And they were not to marry whores nor divorcees,
And any daughters who did whore were to be burnt,

And the senior curator must be well presented at all times,
And he may not leave his tabernacle,
And his wife must be a virgin and also not a foreigner.

And Moses made clear to Aaron that any deformed or defective descendants were not to be given the tabernacle gig, No blind, lame, flat-nosed, extra-limbed, broken-footed, broken-handed, hunchbacked, dwarfed, spotty-eyed, scurvous, scabrous or broken-balled man may ever run my tabernacle.

Leviticus 22

And of course any son of Aaron with leprosy or gonorrhoea or diarrhoea must be stood down from duty,
And if he touches a corpse or some semen or a creeping animal then he must wash,
And generally all the sons of Aaron must keep to the Rules rigidly.

Now of course any slaves owned by Aaron may eat the meat payments,
But daughters who marry out may not unless she is divorced or widowed and returns.

And Aaron insisted that he should only be paid in perfect animals for deformed or scurvous or scabrous ones could be poisonous,
And no castrated animals neither, nor one with damaged balls you no longer want,
None under seven days old,
And no mothers and children to be killed on the same day.

Leviticus 23

And Moses's nation was taking place,
And Moses defined the party days he had previously insti-

gated,

And the fourteenth day of the first month would be to celebrate the Great Escape

And the first day of the seventh month would be a day of rest, signalled by trumpets,

And the tenth day of the same month is to be a Day of Fasting and Reflection

And on the fifteenth day of the seventh month we will go camping in the fields and feast for seven days to celebrate the Harvest.

Leviticus 24

And it came to pass that Aaron performed his duties,

And the people supplied oil for the lamps,

And bread for Aaron and his boys,

And in due course the new Rules were tested,

For a half-Egyptian boy fought with a Hebrew and the half-Egyptian cursed the wretched Hebrews,

And he was stoned to death, as per the rules.

For rigid adherence to the Rules was the only route to discipline and order and the only hope for the Hebrews,

And Moses enforced ruthlessly breach for breach, eye for eye, tooth for tooth: as he hath caused a blemish in a man, so shall it be done to him again.

And the rule of law pertained, and no man was immune,

And the Hebrews acknowledged their leader Moses.

Leviticus 25

But Moses had an itch to scratch,

And Moses moved on to farming,

For a fledgling nation needs self-sufficiency.

And all farm land was to be owned by the state,

And all farm land was to be leased from Jubilee to Jubilee,

And all land transactions are to be based on the date of the Jubilee,

And the price of land is set according to how soon the next Jubilee is,

And if the Jubilee is many years the price will be higher,

And if the Jubilee is near the price will be lower,

For the value of the land is determined by the number of harvests available.

And no land outside of the city walls shall be sold forever,

But shall be leased only until the next Jubilee,

And in this way all men may be provided for.

And who should work the land, but slaves,

And Moses made sure the rules governing slaves were equitable,

And a neighbour who sells himself into slavery will gain his freedom in the year of the Jubilee.

But slaves bought from foreigners shall not gain their freedom, but shall be inherited by the children.

And a neighbour who sells himself to a foreigner may be bought back, calculating the price by the years to the Jubilee,

And in the year of the Jubilee he will be free.

Leviticus 26

And Moses handed down Rule after Rule and Regulation,

And Moses was sure that if the people kept no idols, and stuck to the rest days, and paid off Aaron and ate well, and segregated the sick, and practised sexual continence,

Then the farmwork would be done, and the rains would come, and the land would bear fruit,

And there would be so much grain that they would be threshing until grape harvest,

And so many grapes that they would be busy until time to

sow the grain again,
>And they would have bread and it would be good.

And there would be peace in the land,
>And there would be no wild animals nor bandits,
>And enemies would be repelled.

But idolatry, exotica and incontinence was sure to lead to famine, disease, fever, terror and disaster,
>Your enemies will steal your grain and take your lives,
>Wild beasts will ravage your land, and plagues will strike you down,
>Your children will be killed, your herds destroyed and your highways impassable,
>Your grain will run low, you will eat the flesh of your sons and of your daughters.

And your spirits will be so broken you will fall before your enemies, and you shall wither as slaves,
>But discipline leads to prosperity, so heed these Rules.

Leviticus 27

Numbers

Numbers 1

And the Hebrew nation began to take shape,
 And the erstwhile slaves regained independent discipline,
 And the community melded and cooperated,
 And in the desert unity bloomed.

And Moses recognised the next step was an army,
 And Moses ordered a poll of all males of arms-bearing age;
twenty in those days,
 And there were forty-six thousand and five hundred male
children of Reuben,
 And fifty-nine thousand three hundred of Simeon,
 And forty-five thousand and six hundred and fifty of Gad,
 And seventy four thousand and six hundred of Judah,
 And fifty-four thousand and four hundred of Issachar,
 And fifty-seven thousand and four hundred of Zebulun,
 And forty thousand and five hundred of Joseph,
 And thirty-two thousand and two hundred of Manasseh,
 And thirty-five thousand and four hundred of Benjamin,
 And sixty-two thousand and seven hundred of Dan,
 And forty-one thousand and five hundred of Asher,
 And fifty-three thousand and four hundred of Naphtali.

And Aaron managed to excuse his boys from the army count,
 And Aaron's boys and indeed all their cousins, all Levites,
were to hang around the tabernacle.

Numbers 2

And Moses appointed Captains and camping grounds,
 And the army was structured along family lines,
 And everyone did as they were told.

Numbers 3

And Moses ordered the Levites to obey Aaron,
 And no longer were the firstborn of each family to be sacrificed,
  For Levites were in effect sacrificed en masse,
  Or that was the official story.

And the seven thousand and five hundred children of Gershon were to take care of the tabernacle tent, the covering and the hangings and the curtains,
 And the eight thousand and six hundred children of Kohath were to take care of the sanctuary, the altar, and the candlestick,
 And the six thousand and two hundred children of Merari were to take care of the boards, the bars, the pillars, the sockets and vessels of the tabernacle.

And Aaron squeezed one last concession from Moses,
 For there were more firstborns than there were Levites,
  And for each one five shekels were paid,
  And the money went to Aaron, naturally.

Numbers 10

And the Hebrews did travel through the desert, with Hobab the Midianite as guide,
 And with new silver trumpets to sound the command.

Numbers 11

And the throng wandered the desert replete with rules, customs, regulations and etiquette,
 But no land.

And fires broke out in the camp,
 And the people whinged about their diet,
 And the people fondly recalled Egypt,

And the burden depressed Moses,
And the people begged for meat,
But the new nation's seed flocks and herds could not be killed,
And a passing flock of quails was greedily wolfed,
And the protein made the beggars sick.

Numbers 12

And again Moses came under the cosh,
For Moses enjoyed a bit of exotica and had a charming lady,
And that was fine, but the devil was in the detail,
For the great governor's bit of fluff was not pure Hebrew,
But was a child of Ham, a rather tall and glamorous Ethiopian.

Now, understandably, Moses' choice had been the subject of some discussion,
And Aaron and Miriam spoke up,
But Moses took Miriam and Aaron to the tabernacle,
And Miriam mysteriously left camp for seven days.

Numbers 13

And Moses wanted a homeland,
And Moses instructed a man from each tribe to go on a recce into the land of the Canaanites,
And the team set off and travelled to Hebron via Zin and Rehob,
And they came across the brook of Eschcol,
And found grapes and pomegranates and figs,
And after forty days returned to Moses in Kadesh,
And reported that the land flowed with milk and honey,
And they showed the grapes and pomegranates and figs to the delight of the crowd.

And after the good news came the bad,

And the bad was that the land was populated by the children
of Anak,

And there were walled cities,

And the Hittites and the Jebusites and the Amorites were in
the mountains,

And the Canaanites were by the sea.

And hawkish Caleb stepped from the crowd and urged invasion,

For he felt the people were strong,

But the doves insisted the lands were too great, and the inhab-
itants were giants,

And there was no chance.

Numbers 14

And again the whines were heard from the camp, and the
whinging grew ever stronger, and the ungrateful elements and
the politicking elements and the wannabe leaders fomented
unrest,

And calls rang forth for a new leader, and a return to Egypt,

And Joshua and Caleb spoke up,

And Joshua and Caleb described the glories of the promised
lands,

But Moses turned and led his people toward the Red Sea,
away from the promised lands.

Numbers 16

And then Korah led a party of two hundred and fifty community
leaders,

And demanded why Moses and Aaron were in charge,

And demanded why only Aaron's sons took the meat and
grain payments,

And demanded a slice of that pie.

And Moses saw Dathan and Abiram in the dissenting crowd but

they snubbed him when he called them,

And they demanded why Moses had taken them from the comfort of slavery in Egypt, from a land of milk and honey,

And had not led them to a new land of milk and honey,

And it seemed to them, not without reason, that Moses had led them out of Egypt purely for his own self-aggrandisement.

But Moses was by now a master of control,

And Moses invited all the dissenters to return the following day with their incense burners,

And Moses planned another of his spectaculars.

And the following day dawned and Korah and Dathan and Abiram and their supporters gathered in their tents,

And Moses warned the throng to keep back,

And Moses announced that he would be happy to step aside should anyone show that he was not the right man to take the party forward,

And as he finished speaking an explosion ripped through the air,

And Korah and Dathan and Abiram and their women and their children were ripped into pieces,

And in the smoke and the chaos there was a crater and splintered incense burners,

And Moses ordered the splinters to be collected and beaten into a sheet of brass,

And the sheet was to cover the altar in the tabernacle,

And it was to be a sign unto the children of Israel,

And it was to be a memorial unto the children of Israel that no stranger which is not of the seed of Aaron come near to offer incense in the tabernacle.

But this latest spectacular did not go down well,

And the people were outraged,

But Moses was ready with further manoeuvres,
And the tabernacle was shrouded in smoke,
And the people were afraid,
And Aaron ran riot with his incense burner,
And fourteen thousand and seven hundred died.

Numbers 17

And Moses demanded each tribe to provide a rod with their name on,
 And Aaron provided the Levite rod,
 And Aaron's rod was fresh,
 And as a fresh branch placed in water will bud,
 So Aaron's budded overnight,
 And it was seen that Aaron's rod was superior to those of the remaining eleven tribes, for theirs were old and dead and did not bud.

And it was clear to the throng who was in charge,
 And it was clear that Aaron's sinecure would be defended with all vigour,
 And that punishment for unauthorised approach of the tabernacle would be swift and brutal.

Numbers 20

And in the dessert of Zin, in Kadesh, Miriam of the timbrels did pass away,
 And again the party ran out of water,
 And again there was whining from the camp,
 And whinging ungrateful elements and politicking elements and wannabe leaders fomented unrest,
 And again a spring was dug.

And Moses sent a messenger to Edom,
 And the messenger explained to Edom how they had left their

comfy homes in Egypt for this shithole Kadesh,

And you've got a nice place here, guv, but we won't touch a thing if you let us through,

And Edom, chuckling to himself, wasn't having any of it.

And the Hebrews moved on to mount Hor,

And in mount Hor Aaron passed away,

And Aaron's son Eleazar succeeded him.

Numbers 21

And the Hebrews journeyed on,

And the spies of Arad the Canaanite saw them

And Arad the Canaanite seized some stragglers,

And the Hebrew vengeance was swift and brutal,

And the Canaanite cites were destroyed utterly,

And the place renamed Hormah ("devoted to destruction").

And the Hebrews journeyed on to the Red Sea, skirting Edom,

And in the hardship of the travel whining rose from the camp,

And whinging ungrateful elements and politicking elements and wannabe leaders fomented unrest,

And the people complained about the food and the wilderness and the snakes,

And many died from snakebite.

And the caravan moved on to Oboth and to Ijeabarim and Zared,

And they pitched up on the border between the Amorites and Moab,

And thence to Beer, and Mattanah and Nahaliel and Bamoth and Pisgah.

And from there a messenger was sent to Sihon, king of the Amorites, to request safe passage across his lands,

And the messenger promised not to loot any land nor drink any water,

Do you think I was born yesterday, muttered Sihon,

And Sihon gathered his forces and struck at Jahaz,

But the Hebrew people had grown strong,

And Sihon was destroyed and Sihon's lands from Arnon to Jabbok were taken,

And the Hebrews took the towns and the villages and dwelt in the lands of the Amorites.

And next they turned attention to Og, the king of Bashan,

And Og also fancied his chances against the desert arrivistes,

And Og also was utterly destroyed,

And his lands settled by the Hebrews.

Numbers 22

And the occupying army moved on to the borders of Balak the Moab,

And Balak was worried,

For Balak could not fail to notice the wanton destruction of the Amorites and Bashan,

And Balak summoned a council of Moabites and Midianites,

And pointed out that the Hebrews would in all likelihood wipe the floor with their boys. We need help.

And Balak proposed an envoy to a soldier of fortune of whom he had heard tell,

And Balak spake thus to the council, If you have a problem, if no one else can help, and if you can find him, maybe you can hire... Balaam.

And the council agreed that Balaam could be hired,

And an envoy was dispatched.

And the envoy met with Balaam,

And Balaam laughed and asked, Who do you think you're kidding, these Hebrews are tough nuts and way beyond Balak's boys,

    And the envoy returned,
    And Balak sent a second party,
    And Balaam was brought to Balak.

Numbers 23

And Balaam had a tough job,

    But he knew some Moabite superstitions,
    And Balaam suggested some sacrifices and a speech,
    And Balak thought that a Good Plan,
    And, lo, the cattle were slaughtered,
    And Balaam stood to speak,
    And Balaam stood in the silence and the expectation,
    And the silence pounded in Balaam's head,
    And words of comfort did not come to Balaam,
    And Balaam wondered how one could defy the Hebrews for they were many, and they were vicious,
    But Balak interrupted, What are you saying? You're meant to be on my side.
    And Balaam had not meant to speak his thoughts.

And Balak took Balaam to another field,

    And they could view the Hebrews from the vantage point,
    And a further seven altars were built,
    And a bullock and ram killed on each one,
    And Balaam had another go,
    But again all Balaam could think was that the Hebrew fighting machine was like a bolt of lightning,
    And that the fighting machine would carry on until it had razed every building and sucked every bit of loot from its target,
    And that there really was little point in opposing them,
    And Balak was not amused.

But Balak was prepared to give Balaam one last go,

And seven more altars were built and another lot of animals killed.

Numbers 24

And Balaam admired the Hebrews in their tent city,
And Balaam knew the Hebrews were a people on the make,
And the Hebrews had proved their mettle in the Great Escape,
And the time in the desert had not been wasted,
And Balaam advised Balak to let sleeping dogs lie.

And Balak was, of course, pretty peeved,
And Balak sent Balaam away with no pay,
And it was Balaam's turn to be miffed,
And Balaam insisted his was an impartial independent opinion,
And Balaam pointed out that he hadn't wanted to help in the first place, as he knew then what the answer would be,
But, Since you insist, I'll tell you what is going to happen. A star will come out of Jacob; a sceptre will rise out of Israel. He will crush the foreheads of Moab, the skulls of all the sons of Sheth. Edom will be conquered; Seir, his enemy, will be conquered, but Israel will grow strong. Amalek was first among the nations, but he will come to ruin at last. You're all fucked.

Numbers 25

But the Hebrews did not invade,
For the Moabite women were quite something,
And while the army was encamped the Moabite women tried their luck,
And their luck was good,
And it was all too easy to persuade the superstitious soldiers to get stuck into a spot of sex and idolatry.

And Moses found out,

And the leaders were rounded up and hung out to dry (literally),

And the judges executed every man who screwed a Moabite.

And one man had been out late and was wandering home to his tent,

And on his arm was a rather lovely young thing,

All flashing eyes, long legs and youthful exuberance,

As one of royal blood is expected to be,

And the marriage would have joined two great houses,

And the pair passed the tabernacle,

And as they did Phinehas (son of Eleazar) seized a spear,

And speared the pair of them, her through her belly.

And Moses was not going to tolerate the Moabites,

And a killing spree was loosed,

And twenty-four thousand paid the death penalty for a bit of fluff and the possibility of a peace treaty.

Numbers 26

And Moses instructed Eleazar to count up the soldiers,

And there were forty-three thousand and seven hundred and thirty Reubenites,

And twenty-two thousand two hundred Simeonites,

And forty thousand and five hundred Gadites,

And seventy-six thousand and five hundred of Judah,

And sixty-four thousand and three hundred of Issachar,

And sixty thousand and five hundred of Zebulun,

And of Joseph, fifty-two thousand and seven hundred of Manasseh, and thirty-two thousand and five hundred of Ephraim,

And forty-five thousand and six hundred of Benjamin,

And sixty-four thousand and four hundred of Dan,

And fifty-three thousand and four hundred of Asher,

And forty-five thousand and four hundred of Naphtali,

Totalling six hundred and one thousand, seven hundred and thirty troops.

And loot was to be divided up between the tribes according to the numbers of the tribes,
    And twenty three thousand Levites were also present,
    And among all those men counted there were no escaped slaves remaining,
    And only desert-born men were present; Moses, Joshua and Caleb excepted.

Numbers 27

And Moses decreed that brotherless daughters could inherit,
    For inheritance was on Moses' mind,
    For Moses thought Joshua showed the right stuff to succeed him,
    And Joshua was brought in front of the people and before Eleazar,
    And Moses laid his hands on Joshua,
    And anointed him successor.

Numbers 31

And Joshua took one thousand fighting men from each tribe,
    And Phinehas and Eleazar manned the trumpets,
    And in the wars against the Midianites they killed Evi, Rekem, Zur, Hur, Reba and Balaam,
    And they killed every man of each tribe,
    And they took the children and the women to be slaves and whores,
    And they took the cattle and the sheep,
    And they burnt the cities and castles and contents,
    And returned to parade their gains before Moses.

And Moses was pleased,

And Moses declared that all male prisoners of all ages were to be executed,

And only virgin women prisoners could be kept, all others executed.

And the booty was counted,

And there were six hundred and seventy-five thousand sheep, seventy-two thousand head of cattle, sixty-one thousand asses and thirty-two thousand virgins,

And the Levites were given their cut,

And the non-soldiers were given their cut,

And everyone was happy.

Numbers 32

And the tribes of Reuben and of Gad now had many thousands of cattle,

And the plains east of Jordan were perfect for cattle farming,

And the Reubenites and Gadites rather fancied settling down and farming their cattle,

And they didn't much fancy the stress and strain of invasion and war,

And representatives went to see Moses,

And explained their thoughts.

And Moses was not amused,

For Moses' new vision was one nation with one purpose,

And Moses knew weakness would spread swiftly through the camp,

And Moses gave them a piece of his mind, asking whether they would be happy to sit around scratching their balls while their cousins wiped the blood from their eyes and squinted through the red haze of war,

And Moses made it clear that their secession would ruin the project.

And the Reubenites and Gadites accepted Moses' points,

And suggested they leave their women, and they come fighting until the invasion was complete, and then return to their women in these fields,

It's a deal, said Moses.

And the Reubenites and Gadites and half the Manassehites were given the kingdoms of Sihon and of Og to share,

And they set about building cities.

Numbers 34

And Moses sat down with Joshua and reminded him what the plan was,

And the southern border is from the Dead Sea over Scorpion Pass to the sea in the West,

And the western border is the Mediterranean,

And the north border is from the sea to Mount Hor, through Hamath and Zedad and Ziphron to Hazarenan,

And your eastern border is from Hazarenan through Shepham to Riblah, down the east coast of the Sea of Galilee and down to the Dead Sea.

All this you must conquer and divide up between the tribes.

Deuteronomy

Deuteronomy I

And Moses felt the light was dying,
And Moses girded himself for one last speech,
And Moses stood and started,

Being about to retire finally from public life, I beg leave to offer you my grateful thanks for the many proofs of kindness and confidence which I have received at your hands. It has been my fortune in the discharge of public duties, civil and military, frequently to have found myself in difficult and trying situations, where prompt decision and energetic action were necessary, and where the interest of the people required that high responsibilities should be fearlessly encountered; and it is with the deepest emotions of gratitude that I acknowledge the continued and unbroken confidence with which you have sustained me in every trial. My public life has been a long one, and I cannot hope that it has at all times been free from errors; but I have the consolation of knowing that if mistakes have been committed they have not seriously injured the nation I so anxiously endeavoured to serve, and at the moment when I surrender my last public trust I leave this great people prosperous and happy, in the full enjoyment of liberty and peace, and honoured and respected by every nation of the world.

I leave you as a nation on the brink of great things. We have come together through the trial and tribulations of the exodus from Egypt and the wandering in the desert; we have forged new laws to live by and the identity of our nation has emerged from the crucible of the desert. We have passed by Seir and by

Ar, and been stung by the Amorites and smitten the Sihonites. We destroyed Og of Bashan and divided his lands and we have looked upon Canaan and mapped out our future. Your future lies in Joshua's hands, charge Joshua and encourage him and strengthen him and he shall cause you to inherit the land you see. Take care not to undermine nor to secede from Joshua's leadership. What have you to gain by division and dissension? Delude not yourselves with the belief that a breach once made may be afterwards repaired. If the nation is once severed, the line of separation will grow wider and wider, and the controversies which are now debated and settled by debate will then be tried in fields of battle and determined by the sword. Neither should you deceive yourselves with the hope that the first line of separation would be the permanent one, and that nothing but harmony and concord would be found in the new associations formed upon the dissolution of this nation. Local interests would still be found there, and unchastened ambition. And if the recollection of common dangers, in which the people of this nation stood side by side against the common foe, the memory of victories won by their united valour, the prosperity and happiness they have enjoyed under the present Laws, the proud name they bear as citizens of this great nation—if all these recollections and proofs of common interest are not strong enough to bind us together as one people, what tie will hold united the new divisions of empire when these bonds have been broken and this nation dissevered ? The first line of separation would not last for a single generation; new fragments would be torn off, new leaders would spring up, and this great and glorious nation would soon be broken into a multitude of petty States, without commerce, without credit, jealous of one another, armed for mutual aggression, loaded with taxes to pay armies and leaders, seeking aid against each other from foreign powers, insulted and trampled upon by other nations, until, harassed with conflicts and humbled and debased in spirit, they would be ready to submit to the absolute dominion of any military adventurer and to surrender their liberty for the sake of repose.

But in order to maintain the nation unimpaired it is absolutely necessary that the laws passed by me should be faithfully executed in every part, and that every good citizen should at all times stand ready to put down, with the combined force of the nation, every attempt at unlawful resistance, under whatever pretext it may be made or whatever shape it may assume. But the laws cannot be maintained nor the nation preserved, in opposition to public feeling, by the mere exertion of the coercive powers confided to the General Government. The foundations must be laid in the affections of the people, in the security it gives to life, liberty, character, and property in every quarter of the country, and in the fraternal attachment which the citizens bear to one another as members of one family, mutually contributing to promote the happiness of each other. Even those citizens who must be exiled must not be cast away entirely – Bezer, Ramoth and Golan shall be set aside as a safe harbour for exiles of our nation so they might not be at the mercy of alien powers.

Deuteronomy 5

And that should really have been that, but Moses being Moses and feeling power slipping from his grasp felt compelled to give some last pointers and recaps and caveats.

And Moses commenced with a recap of the commandments;

And always recall that we are the Hebrew nation, which has come out of the land of Egypt, out of the house of bondage, we are of pure blood and these are the rules by which we shall live.

We shall not corrupt our purity nor bow down nor serve any other master; for we are the Hebrew nation.

We shall visit the iniquity of them that stray from our identity upon the children unto the third and fourth generation. But those that remain within the bosom of the nation shall know our mercy.

We shall not take the name of our nation in vain, and we will not hold him guiltless that doth take our name in vain.

We shall honour our fathers and our mothers, and our days shall belong upon the land which the nation shall grant unto us.

We shall remember every seventh day is for rest. Six days we shall labour, and do all our work. But the seventh day is the day of rest: in it no man may force labour, nor shall we force labour on our son, nor our daughter, nor our manservant, nor our maidservant, nor our cattle, nor any stranger that is within our gates.

We shall not kill.
    We shall not commit adultery.
    We shall not steal.
    We shall not bear false witness against our neighbour, nor shall we covet our neighbour's house, nor our neighbour's wife, nor his manservant, his maidservant, his ox, his ass, nor any thing that is our neighbour's.

Remember these rules when you are in cities thou buildest not; and houses full of all good things which thou fillest not; and wells digged thou diggest not; and vineyards and olive trees which thou plantest not; when thou shalt have eaten and be full – beware lest you forget the laws and the identity which brought you there out of the land of Egypt, out of bondage.

    Remember them and make sure your children remember them, and their children unto eternity. And when thy son asketh thee in time to come, saying, What means the testimonies and the statutes and the judgments then thou shalt say unto thy son, we were the Pharaoh's bondsmen in Egypt and Moses brought us out of Egypt with great leadership and he brought us here and forged us as a nation and left us on the brink of greatness.

And Moses recapped the next most important Rules and recommended that false prophets be killed and heathen cities destroyed and abominations stoned to death.

And Moses went over a last bit of military strategy and explained that newlyweds, new farmers and cowards need not fight,

And nations should be offered vassaldom rather than destroying them straight up,

And in destruction be careful not to destroy useful stuff, like olive trees.

And, warming to his theme, Moses had a last finger wagging about general day to day life, banning cross dressing, bastards, eunuchs, Ammonites and Moabites; exhorting the people to dig holes for their shit and not play with whores nor sodomites.

And Moses did rant and rant and lecture and moralise until finally he was done and finished with, For I know that after my death ye will utterly corrupt yourselves and turn aside from the way I have commanded you and evil will befall you in the latter days because you will do evil, and Moses took his book of Rules and placed it in the Ark and handed the reins to Joshua, singing a final paean as he did.

And Moses and maybe Joshua with him went up the mountain of Nebo to survey the future lands of the nation,

And Moses' eye was not dim nor his natural force abated,

And yet Moses did not return from that trip
And his body was never found,
And Joshua, unconstrained by Moses, took the reins.